To
Timothy.
Kirkpatrick
From
Elder Richard Harris

God
Bless
You
Richard

BETTER
not
BITTER

Elder Richard H. Harris, Jr

authorHOUSE®

AuthorHouse™
1663 Liberty Drive
Bloomington, IN 47403
www.authorhouse.com
Phone: 1 (800) 839-8640

Published by AuthorHouse 12/07/2015

ISBN: 978-1-5049-1013-2 (sc)
ISBN: 978-1-5049-1012-5 (hc)
ISBN: 978-1-5049-1011-8 (e)

Library of Congress Control Number: 2015906865

Dedication

To Jesus Christ who is my Lord and Savior, My Hope, Rock, Counselor, Advocate, Inspiration, and Strength.,

In memory of my parents, Richard H. Harris, Sr.
and Odessa Harris Powell;

to my five sons, Damean, M., Richard H. III, Duane R., Brandon L., Bryan M., and my precious daughter, Brittany R. Harris, all of whom have been a driving force of strength and a determining factor for me to evolve into a better man, person, and father. Although it is God who changes the individual and the individual who decides to walk with God, you, my children, are all significant factors in my desire to change. Thanks for your support, encouragement, forgiveness, and love.

Acknowledgments

There are a bevy of interesting and wonderful people who enhanced and enlightened my quality of life in a variety of ways. Their contributions enabled and empowered me to write this book. Although this journey has been long and tedious and still developing, I thank God for all that has transpired-- the good and the bad. Being saved, delivered, and filled with the Holy Ghost, did not exempt me from daily trials, tests, temptations, persecutions, tribulations, and long suffering. My vision for writing this book came during my incarceration. I trusted God to change, challenge, and make me over. I choose to be **better** not **bitter.** During this holding pattern in life, my faith was set in motion; God took out my stony heart and replaced it with a heart of flesh. God slowly allowed the walls of rejection, abandonment, loneliness, hatred, and selfishness to dissipate.

To the innumerable people who helped through prayer, patience, words of encouragement, and even attitudes I say, "Thank you and I thank God for you!!"

Contents

Foreword

The integrity of Richard Harris lies in the fact that he is open to growth. As his Pastor of 5 years, I have challenged that statement on many occasions and he has never caused me to regret doing so. He walked into ministry secure enough in himself to withstand every degree of difficulty and to receive correction without feeling that his character had been flawed nor his intelligence challenged. I can say with great assurance that he is a baptized believer of Jesus Christ and he is definitely filled with the presence of the Holy Ghost. He is an example of a man who has journeyed through life with hope and the Favor of God.

The life experiences he shares in this book will serve as a guide to those who are without hope. It shows that through God all things are possible and that each and every situation we encounter in life is beneficial. I'm thankful to God that Elder Richard Harris possesses the courage to expose and unveil his life and to be transparent to the world for the sake of the Kingdom.

His statements from this book, "Prison had become a school of higher learning for me..., it is profound to me to know I am going to be dead longer than I will be alive", are thought provoking and encouraging to me as Senior Pastor to The Enon Church, Atlanta, Georgia.

Favor may come with a cost but God's salvation is free to anyone who confesses His Name. This a testament that one can be locked up but most certainly not locked OUT of Christ. Elder Harris' life story is a testament to God's favor and His salvation. In my thirty five years of preaching, twenty four of those years as a pastor, I have read a great deal of literature on every level and area of ministry. However, I have never encountered anyone who makes it as plain, practical and principled as Elder Richard Harris Jr. I believe the words contained here in this book will transform and catapult each reader to a higher personal dimension in the Lord Jesus Christ.

Dr. Gregory L. Pollard, Senior Pastor

The Enon Church

Preface

I began writing this book in early April, 1995 while a prisoner in body, mind, and soul. I was saved and delivered from self, drugs, and alcohol on January 1, 1994. At the time, I was already one year physically incarcerated for a 1993 felonious assault charge for which I'd been convicted on March 4, 1994. At age 43, this was my first and last incarceration, only by the grace of God through His son, Jesus Christ, my Lord and Savior.

I can say without equivocation that the Bible's role in my life is paramount. My way of thinking and living without the Bible empowered my sin, weighty burdens, and erratic behavioral patterns. This mindset and tumultuous cycle which began from birth, set in motion my worldly choices and decisions. Forty-three years into worldly deception which included parental fighting/divorces, being thrust into parental roles and social introversion was hard. My battle was with self, alcohol, drugs, and societal interaction. Interwoven challenges with a prejudice work environment, unhealthy marriages, manhood accountability/responsibility, death of familial/friends, and prison time had made me exceedingly weary.

This book addressed how the issues of sex, money, alcohol, drugs, and a host of other sinful ways affected my life and the lives of those around me. The book explores deeply how my heart issues, wilderness mentality, and environmental issues along with traditional and cultural upbringing collided. Then, these pages disclose the dynamics of my ongoing change process by renewing my mind through Holy Scriptures.

Because its foundation is the Holy Bible, this book is intended to unite and engage the reader with Holy Scriptures. The purpose is to bring empowerment, enlightenment, enhancement and renewed hope toward restoration with God. I have spent over fifteen years preparing this book and forty-five years experiencing it. My ultimate heart's desire is that this labor will, in some way, bring glory to God and uplift someone misinformed.

God gave me the alone time I needed to complete this book, without the distractions of a wife and young children. I wrote the bulk of it in prison and spare moments while in college for seven years. I planned to finish it after my associate's degree in 2004, but God blessed me to complete two more degrees.

"Therefore seeing we have this ministry, as we have received mercy, we faint not;" (2Cor. 4:1 KJV). The time away from Church, volunteering and extended family was difficult but the personal time with God, contemplation, and writing proved fruitful. The seeds for this book were planted through self-motivation, life experiences, and my willingness to help others with similar situations. I've come to understand you cannot help others with the same mind-set I once owned, but since renounced. *"But have renounced the hidden things of dishonesty, not walking in craftiness, nor handling the word of God deceitfully; but by manifestation of the truth commending ourselves to every man's conscience in the sight of God." (2Cor.4:2 KJV)*

Finally, my ministry has reached very diverse audiences in terms of age, religious persuasion, educational levels, and social backgrounds. Struggles are not respecter of persons, so neither am I. I have sought to write this book without specific readers intended. It is my prayer that God through Jesus Christ, richly blesses everyone who reads the pages that follow.

There are no secrets in Christ Jesus *"What fruit had ye then in those things whereof ye are now ashamed? (Romans 6:21a KJV).* I am grateful to have undertaken God's Word realizing he has paid for my sin, shame, and guilt. The Bible is specific on three things one must do to broaden spiritual maturity.

Then Jesus said to his disciples, "If any man will come after Me, let him deny himself, and take up his cross, and follow Me." (Matthew 16:24 KJV)

I protest by your rejoicing which I have in Christ Jesus our Lord, I die daily." *(1 Corinthians 15:31 KJV)*

"Humble yourselves therefore under the mighty hand of God, that He may exalt you in due time." (1 Peter 5: KIV6)

It saddens me that many Christians are not taught these Biblical principles which are required daily for one's daily spiritual development. In addition, it gives me great encouragement that I can write with the veracity of God's word through my witness.

Jesus saith unto him, "I am the way, the truth, and the life: No man cometh unto the Father but by me. If ye had known me, ye should have known my Father also. And henceforth ye know Him and have seen Him." (John 14:6-7 KJV).

I retired from an industry that manufactured light in the natural sense to every household, business, and dark places (street lights, etc.). I now commit to supplying spiritual illumination which is greater and more essential to life.

"Then spake Jesus again unto them, saying, I am the light of the world: He that followeth me shall not walk in darkness, but shall have the light of life." (John 8:12 KJV).

I understand I cannot go back to the way I used to do things, there is no future going back. My life and ministry are dependent on the enabling power and renewing power of God in Christ Jesus. *"I am crucified with Christ: nevertheless I live; yet not I, but Christ liveth in me: and the life which I now live in the flesh I live by faith of the Son of God, who loved me, and gave himself for me"*(Galatians 2:20 KJV).

My Childhood: Tears and Bad Memories

At the ripe age of 43, I was removed from society for the first time ever. The physical freedom I was accustomed to having was gone, but my spiritual liberty would be born and my mind renewed. Incarceration presented new challenges in my life. Not excluding pain, hurt, and other feelings, but allowing God to change my thoughts, words, actions, habits and character. In April, 1995, I was inspired to write about my life experiences. I'd done a year on my bit (prison time) which consisted of a three-year gun specification and 5 to 15 years on the felonious assault. In layman's terms, I could be released after serving three years and a third of the 5 to 15. It does suffice to say, I had plenty of time to reflect.

Although my memory is still somewhat hazy from years of alcohol, drug, and other substance abuse it's easy to remember pain. Unwanted feelings and pain started for me very early in life. The pain of my early years nested in Ma and Dad's bedroom which resembled an adult battleground. I shed many hidden tears between the ages of 7 and 15 years old. Most times, their bedroom door was shut. The violence in my parents' bedroom which manifested in verbal, physical, and emotional attacks could be heard all over the house. Their room was filled with cussing, unidentifiable but disturbing noises, accompanied quite often with the sounds of physical fighting. While we kids could hear what was going on, looking inside was off-limits.

I felt a sense of hopelessness because I wanted to defend my mother, but was fearful of my dad. It was hard to understand why dad was beating her, but it soon became our family's normal.

Although as I describe each individuals room it's because each had a particular affect on me. We moved for revitalization purposes around 1960 I was 10 years old with an older sister 13 and, three younger brothers, 9, 5 and 4 and my baby sister will be born seven years later. I heard my dad more than I saw him because he worked crazy swing shift hours in the steel mill. So I would only see him come and go to work occasionally. At times, he would drop off a box of donuts or a gallon of ice cream for us to eat. I grew to accept his absence in my life, at sporting and school events, at the dinner table, and most of all, a loving presence of a father.

On the other hand, I interacted with Ma every day. She drank beer everyday, cooked and baked wonderfully, cussed like a sailor, and was very protective of her children. Ma fulfilled some of Dad's gaps, teaching me about personal hygiene as well as sexually transmitted diseases. I could talk to her about anything, except for what was going on between her and my dad.

We lived in a predominantly black neighborhood with a few sprinklings of other ethnic groups. The homes in our community were close to each other. The front yards were small; the back lots were narrow (about 60 feet long and 30 feet wide). Our four bedroom house was three houses away from the main street, so we heard the constant comings and goings of car and foot traffic. The high visibility of our house led to many quarrels and fights with neighbor kids over trespassing, balls, rocks, objects being tossed back and forth over the fence and even broken windows. I was often a part of these quarrels trying to defend my brothers. As the oldest brother, I did not want to convey any softness or fear. Fulfilling my role as the tough older brother against the seven neighborhood boys, some older some younger, was a handful. As a result, the backyard became more of a combat zone than play area. It was similar to my parents'bedroom, a territorial battle ground, though there was a number of escape options outside.

My older sister enjoyed the privacy of her own bedroom in front of the house along the driveway. My two other brothers shared a room across from me. My brothers' room was for playing, drawing, and brotherly fights. I shared a room with my brother, who was a year younger, in the back of the house along our driveway. We could peer out our window into the neighbor's bed and bathroom. These rooms had their own affect on my perspective on things. My room was akin to a voyeuristic retreat because the neighbors seldom closed the curtains and never the blinds. This is where I experienced puberty and my first mysterious sexual event. Arousal and ejaculation were scary as well as tearful. I dare not share this puzzling incident. I did not understand what was happening or what the subject matter was. I would have to believe this is when sin and youthful lust entered my life. Going to bed faithfully was easy just to watch the neighbor woman brought newfound excitement. For me, the upstairs of this home brought many tears, bad memories, and negative feelings. I felt trapped with no escape route and forced to hear abuse, hatred, and discontent between my parents. I now often wonder, where was the love.

I had already formed my own perception of what a beautiful woman looked liked. One of my elementary teachers was tall, appeared to have smooth skin and a light caramel brown complexion, with long dark curly Indian-type hair. She wore glasses extremely soft spoken, and carried herself like no other woman I had encountered. Her legs were perfectly shaped, and her clothes always form-fitting. She was a polite and good teacher, which made going to school easy. She represented my young vision of beauty.

I began to experience sensual desires between ages eight and ten. Ma left us with a first time neighborhood babysitter, a mature, larger, very voluptuous woman who, on that day, had evidently been drinking. Her walk and breath said it all. I was the only one home when this woman fell asleep on our couch. Noticing a considerable part of her chest area was exposed, my interest was piqued and aroused. I sat on the floor near the living room entrance gawking for the longest time. Pretty soon, watching wasn't enough so I crept slowly up and began to touch what my eyes had seen. This feeling appeared to control me and lasted way long after my observation. Fearing there could be consequences if she awoke or someone walked in, I retreated outside to play. I knew alcohol had played a part in her slumbering instead of babysitting. Although I didn't get caught, I was aroused by those sexual feelings. I also realized how alcohol played a role in my so called babysitter's ability to do her job. Little did I know how much this experience would mark my life and character?

The sound of violence was not the only sound we heard in my house. Music and other forms of entertainment were present too. We listened to oldies on a 33 and 78 rpm turntable in the dining room. Dad had fruit crates

4

of jazz albums; Ma preferred gospel, rock & roll, and comedy records. We also had a pool table which Dad had bought and assembled in the dining room. It seemed to consume the whole area and some shots were impossible.

In contrast, our living room had very little light or life. The picture window allowed minimal sunlight to come in which kept the room dim. The corner window which was constructed higher was even less luminous.

I'll never forget watching Dad's second or third professional boxing match on our 25-inch black and white television. Ma had friends, children, and neighbors over. It was late evening and food (chicken), cards, and alcohol were present. The smell of food and alcohol was always prevalent in our home. After Dad won the fight, the eating, drinking and card playing continued. People would give my brothers and me money to dance and clown. They laughed, drank, gossiped, cussed, and played cards incessantly.

Alcohol was a main stay in our home. I don't remember Dad ever indulging, but everybody else did and appeared to enjoy it. I could detect Dad was not a party guy or avid drinker; he seemed to have other things on his mind. When he came home from the fight, he seemed humble not gaudy. When he came in, he appeared to be taking the temperature of his surroundings. And soon after, the party people began dispersing. I perceived that Dad didn't want to be around the company Ma kept. Ma and Dad did not associate with the same people. She had her friends; he had his and very few.

Drinking was traditional and culturally accepted before wakes, before funerals, at family gathering, on fishing trips, at holiday events, and while playing cards. As young as four, I can remember being given beer. This "tradition" continued with my younger brothers. The alcohol was intended to curb their hyperactivity and stopped them from rocking back in forth on the couch and recliner. In reality, this custom caused me to crave alcohol whenever it was presented to me.

At one point, Dad owned a Doberman Pincher which was fenced in the back of the yard. This dog, whose name I can't recall, was sleek black with a distinct shade of copper brown running from his chest to his neck. He had white teeth with two prolonged on the top and bottom jaws and always appeared to be extremely vicious. My brothers, the neighborhood kids nor I played or went anywhere near where the dog lived. Like my Dad, the dog seemed to be a loner. Dad never hung out with others and I was afraid to approach either one of them. Dad at times had to use a stick to push the dog's pan of food to him while standing at the gate. Other times he had to punch the dog under his mouth awfully hard to get him to obey. I was fearful of the dog and my dad. My dad was a no-nonsense and an authoritative parent; the dog was just plain scary.

For as long as I can remember, my siblings and I had chores. In later years, doing these tasks would enhance my work ethic and independence. Ma not only demanded that we clean up our rooms, but also that we clean anything we messed up in her whole house. One time, Ma had told me to wash the dishes and clean the kitchen before she came home. Instead, I decided to go out and play street football after we ate dinner, my sister had cooked. When she came home and the chores were not done, she said she was going to tell Dad. I dreaded the thought not because Dad had ever whipped me before but I was intimidated by this no nonsense man. When he came home, he summoned me to go into the cellar and "get like I came into the world" (naked). I was terrified because this had never happened before. He came downstairs carrying a one and half inch thick black belt and gave me the shortest briefing imaginable. I ran for cover. That was the biggest mistake in my young life because before I knew it, he'd caught me and tied me to a steel beam and commenced to beat me. Dad was short, but very strong and powerful. Ma had to run downstairs to get him off me. I fainted, turned black and blue, and don't remember if I went to the hospital or how I recovered. But I do remember Ma telling Dad don't ever whip him like that again. I think he was ashamed of himself. Our relationship was more marred as I avoided him after that. Dad instilled right and wrong in us and was a stern believer once was all he was going to tell us. This one and only whipping was one I would never forget.

Ma was more lenient even though she was loud and boisterous when scolding us. As little boys, we could get away with being disobedient a couple of times. Then Ma disciplined us sternly using a switch, belt, broom handle or anything else that was available. Her beatings were accompanied by profanity. Ma did, however, allow us to be typical boys. We could fall, scrape body parts, throw things, climb trees, and other normal boy stuff.

Ma was a pretty woman just like Gran-ma and my three aunties and all Gran-ma's sisters. She was slender, agile as a doe, and the apple of my eye. To be sure, these tender attributes were not to be taken for weakness for she was also as bold as a lion. I never detected in her any fear. Like Dad, Ma didn't take any mess, but she was always there for us.

On the other hand, Dad never once attended a game or event I participated in. He didn't even come to one of my team's three championship football games. I wanted nothing more than to perform for my dad. I have since accepted and forgiven him, but even today I have scars from the wounds caused by my Dad's absence. You see, Dad was my god. Ma was there cheering me on, hollering, "Don't hit my baby" but I missed my dad, and wished he'd been there to share my love for sports.

Sports were a large part of my life—a part of life I wished I could share with my dad. I played football from ages 7 to 12, and boxed for a year. But my first love was basketball despite my height. I thought you had to be a certain height to play basketball. I admired players like Tiny Nate Archibald, who gave me the incentive to walk on the court and not face rejection because of my height. I had to find a way to fit in and on the court. So I worked particularly hard to learn to use both hands to dribble and shoot the ball as well as hustle.

When I wasn't playing sports, I engaged in other neighborhood activities and rituals. Activities like roaming the streets, going to the open end market a few blocks from home were common. I often went swimming and to the neighborhood playground. Hustling day old bakery goods and walks to my grandparents' house on the opposite side of town were routine as well. All in all, my childhood was good.

I can't remember a time when I didn't have some sort of job. From ages 10 to 15, I hustled aluminum and other precious metals which I had gotten from dilapidated homes and buildings which were being demolished to make way for freeways and other new developments. I also kept money in my pocket by walking elderly neighbor's dogs, going to the store for them, cutting grass, and shoveling snow. I developed a fairly large clientele. I had a paper route at fourteen, and by age fifteen, I got a work permit and started my first "real" job at age sixteen.

I loved sports and money, but other than that I did not know where my life was headed. I certainly realize now that all choices have consequences, be they good or bad.

I was a good student in junior high school, but only because my parents said so. The meaning or purpose for going to school was vague. Ma and Dad had not finished school, they just worked hard. In school, I was more focused on sports than anything else. So when I found out my junior high didn't have a football team, my motivation to attend school was lessened. I thought to myself, "What am I going to do?" I tried out for the track team along with many of my football colleagues whom I had played with or against in the past. Unfortunately, my time of eleven some odd seconds in the one hundred yard dash wasn't good enough, and I did not make the team. I felt a strong sense of rejection. I especially felt my father's absence at this time because I needed his guidance and encouragement.

I decided not to try out for the junior high basketball team fearing that competing against much bigger and taller boys would result in another bout with rejection. My "plan B" was to tryout for intramural basketball league because I just knew there would be more than enough teams and spots to play on. To my surprise, I didn't make that team either. I was a winner and not accustomed to sports rejection or being denied an opportunity to play.

Rejection was by far the worse feeling I experienced while growing up. I also struggled with hatred, abandonment, loneliness, jealousy, and resentment. I didn't leave these feelings at the door when I entered the classroom. I sat in the back of class, afraid to stand up, be called upon and to share in school work. I believed I didn't have what it took to engage intellectually with others. I lacked any expectations for myself as a student. So I began to act out through actions like capping--- talking about people--or their family members. It didn't matter whether we knew the family or not. These practices consumed much of my energy as I began to defend and engaged myself in junior high. I did not like to be put down or talked about. Therefore, I had to make sure I talked about others in ways that kept them from making me their target. Many of these capping episodes led to fist fights and hurt feelings. I grew up in the age of the Temptations "A man ain't supposed to cry", so I suppressed the feelings which grew from my experiences at school.

I first experienced feelings of hatred in the seventh grade. Some boys including a popular athlete were throwing snowballs. I wasn't playing with them, but I ended up getting hit with one of the heavy, gravel-laden snowballs in my left eye. To show just how strong the impact was, I was on the opposite side of street from where the boys were playing. Needless to say, the impact was so severe; I was taken back to school and then rushed to the hospital emergency room. The doctor determined I had a severe hemorrhage and may even lose my left eye vision. While I feared losing my vision, I also hated this older supposedly role model, whom I had admired for his speed. After the incident, my mother and I went to his parents' home. They were apologetic, but deep down inside I still wanted to fight him. This incident caused bitterness and hatred. It was also the reason my dad did not allow my brothers and me to throw things (with the exception of sports balls). Dad did not want to be responsible for us putting someone's eye out or breaking somebody's windows.

While I found a sense of pride in my athletic accomplishments and abilities as well as in social interactions with my football teammates; most of my experiences in junior high did little to build my self-esteem. In fact, some of the teasing I experienced made me believe I had physical abnormalities. Especially while being made fun of during my eighth and ninth grade classes. In the eighth grade a capping classmate would often ask "Did you find that lion that scratched you in the back of your head?" Unconscious of the scar, I asked Ma how I had gotten it. She told me when I was four that I'd fallen out of the back seat of the car and hit my head. Even more embarrassing was when a ninth grade gym classmate hollered over to me in the shower, "You only have one testicle." My mother told me I'd been born that way. These events, while seemingly minor, had an effect on me and made me wonder what other things my parents had kept from me. Some of these thoughts influenced my emotions as well as behaviors.

One last memory of junior high was the assassination of President John F. Kennedy. This historic event was announced over the P.A. system while we were in art class. We were overcome with great sadness. We paused for a moment of silence and were then released for the rest of day.

When I entered high school, my goal was to play football again. I was extremely excited about the football sign-up and try-outs. The day-long turnout was huge and included most of my little league teammates.

The head coach appeared to have already hand-picked certain players. I believed we should have all been allowed to tryout on equal footing. When my name was called, the coach told me I was too small to play any of the available positions. Though I only was one-hundred and thirty-five pounds soaking wet, I had heart and could take and give contact. This experience triggered rejection once again. The coach's favoritism revealed to me how unfair life can be.

I was forced to accept the fact that life is neither equal nor fair. This also marked the end to my football career. While I explored boxing, I then began to turn my focus away from sports and instead became fixated on girls, sex, money, and clothes as well as alcohol, drugs, and gambling. This was my way of fitting in socially and finding my identity. Seeking a sense of self and independence, I was drawn to an older and diverse crowd. The player, pimp, thieves, and con-artist types welcomed me with open arms with the motive of recruiting me to engage in their life styles.

My first blow with death came while riding in a car with three of my shoplifting buddies. When the cops attempted to pull us over, the driver sped away; the cops pursued. When we rounded a corner, we jumped out the car. Everyone went their way, but the police shot at me hitting the tree next to where I stood momentarily. Then I continued running and was able to slip into a friend's house where I stayed for several hours. At that time I called it pure luck that I was not hit by a bullet that day.

I was going to school, hustling and working out half-heartedly as a novice boxer. Dad had warned me that boxing or any sport activity with alcohol, drugs, and women didn't mix. I had heard that advice before in little league. But this time, overcome by curiosity I didn't heed the advice. In the tenth grade, I felt I had to prove myself to a different group of people. I had lost my love of football as well as the circle of friends with whom I had played.

By now I am fifteen; my parents had divorced seemingly out of the blue. The divorce left me blaming and wondering what I had done. I looked up one day and Dad was gone completely. He didn't even come support my boxing debut, which was painful despite the fact that it was short-lived due to my lifestyle and the fact that I didn't like getting punched in the face.

I had one novice Golden Glove moment, but not without conflict. My first and only fight was against a twenty-three year old open (experienced) boxer. At only 16 years old, I was scared. The standing room only crowd didn't help my anxiety not to mention that I wasn't in the best shape because of my lifestyle. I was told at age fifteen; I could only have a certain number of fights before I was moved from novice to open status. The guy I fought had been around awhile and was 23 years old. Each fight was scheduled for three rounds of three minutes. While watching numerous fights before mine was scheduled, I saw much blood from cuts and many teeth flying. As a result, I approached the fight with fear and a lack of confidence. The first round was a feel out round and I sensed he was just as fearful as I. We exchanged numerous punches. After Round 2, it was clear to me that I was not ready. The crowd was not as enthusiastic during the second round as we did more circling than boxing. My goal was to get out of the dark smoked filled high school gymnasium and hot ring with glaring lights. The fear of being knocked out caused me not to answer the third round bell, wishing to spare myself this embarrassment. At that moment, it was clear to me that boxing was not for me. I was still unclear about what my calling was.

It was the 1960s, the era during which riotous activity was prevalent. I didn't know where my place was in this mix. Since the divorce, I had also taken on a parental role with my sister and brothers and helped Ma. In tenth grade, I dealt with role confusion, mixed feelings/ideas, and how I fit into society. My identity was also crippled by the negative activities and behaviors I had assumed. While it wasn't my natural personality, I felt the need to form a harder exterior, a tough don't take no mess mentality. This way of acting would become habitual.

The eleventh grade would define my life for the next twenty-five years. During this year, I began experimenting with a long list of drugs I would try by age twenty one. Even though alcohol and marijuana were my substances of choice, I experimented with speed, pills (uppers/downers), LSD, powder cocaine, nasal inhaler (whistle), airplane glue, angel dust, and embalming fluid. I wasn't introduced to crack cocaine until age thirty three but I stayed in its hellish bondage for ten years until my encounter with Jesus, deliverance, salvation, and being filled with the Holy Spirit.

I had learned cuss words at an early age from Ma, but during the 11th grade, I began using them regularly. I used profanity to defend myself and my siblings, to keep people away from me, and to cut people emotionally. Developing a defensive mind set empowered me and helped me meet specific needs. Because I lived in a mob town with steel workers galore, being on the defensive seemed normal and became familiar.

I encountered one break in the unfamiliar during my junior year. Juniors and seniors were invited to apply for the new Occupational Work Experience (O.W.E.), a work-study program. To participate, participants had to maintain a 2.5 G.P.A. as well as show a strong work ethic. I was the first student selected and accepted. While enrolled, I went to school in the morning and then hurried downtown to begin work at noon. Weekdays, I worked from noon to four and all day Saturday bussing tables and preparing rooms for guests at the Pick Ohio Hotel. I was paid a regular wage and earned as much in tips as I possibly could. Two months after beginning the program, I was promoted to the head waiter position and was given the authority to hire twenty bus boys. The leadership skills and work ethic I attained were priceless. I hired many of my football teammates and others. We worked the main dining doom, ballroom, as well as an array of smaller rooms for special events including those hosted by the Rotary Club and the Chamber of Commerce and other prominent professionals. Before I hung up my boxing gloves, I would leave work to train at the boxing facility in an adjacent downtown area.

Life was good. I earned money every day, and wore flamboyant clothes. I even had suits and pants tailor made so I could "represent" in school or wherever else I went. I stopped going to the gym to train, opting for the burlesque club around the corner where I watched older women dancing. At that point, sexual fantasies were being formed in my mind and I was drinking more alcohol along with a little cough syrup. I continued smoking marijuana to medicate some feelings and to fit in with the worldly crowd. Yes, eleventh grade was where my alcohol and drug addiction began to take root as well as my aggressive tendencies. These were all choices I made, but they were clearly influenced by the environment in which I lived. Addiction and aggressiveness took root in my life, and would fester there for many years.

When I reached my senior year, I just knew I was a shoe-in for best dressed male. After all, being flamboyant was easy for me and was something I enjoyed and worked hard at. Even though I felt I paved the way for fine dress, I came in second place to someone who played football, and interacted daily with the Caucasian kids. I hired him at the hotel, and felt he had begun to emulate my style. Once again, doubt and rejection reared its ugly head and I felt as though I didn't fit in with the class of 1968.

Despite this defeat, I still considered myself a leader. My tutor and boss, Betty, who believed in me, kept me focused. I could sense her genuine interest in me. Despite her stern manner, she encouraged me daily. She used positive reinforcement to mold my work ethic, leadership, and public relation skills.

The hotel and Betty offered me an opportunity to go to cooking school in Switzerland, all expenses paid. I was about to graduate in a few months, and had a big decision to make. I was honored to have been made the offer. But, I decided I would graduate and head for the steel mills where I was assured of earning thirteen dollars or more per hour. I had connections at many of the mills as most of my male family members worked there. They appeared to be living well. Perhaps my life's purpose was to follow in their footsteps. Maybe, I would become the loving supportive father figure like the one I so desperately longed for in my own dad. I didn't yet fully understand the feeling of rejection, abandonment, and loneliness caused by my dad's absence. While I never felt his love, I missed his presence nonetheless. As I saw, it was up to me to survive and bear the elements of the streets all by myself.

Youngstown (known as Y-Town or Little Chicago) was a booming steel town. Many migrated there for the steel jobs. The town was also notorious for mobsters, drugs, and gambling. I entered the lifestyle easily, spending much of my time on the corners, and in pool halls and bars. While, I wasn't "legal age," I did many of the things my grown buddies did. After graduating high school, I wanted to become a full-fledged man. I held my hotel job for a few more months before being hired by United States Steel as a brakeman for their railroad. I turned eighteen two months after graduation; my rite to passage was complete. By this time, I was still drinking alcohol and cough syrup, and smoking. I didn't know it at the time, but I was already entertaining unfamiliar, lying, and perverse spirits through the usage of alcohol and pharmaceuticals.

I loved drugs I could control, not drugs that controlled me. I used drugs that concealed my feelings of hurt, abandonment, loneliness, and rejection. I continued to explore new drugs, and tried paper acid. After using the acid, I went to Modina Garden's Bar and ordered a beer. While pulling change from my pocket to pay for the beer, I experienced my first hallucination. The change began to revolve. I turned toward the pool table light behind me to correct my vision but the hallucinations increased. The pool balls appeared to be dancing to jukebox music. Then suddenly I heard someone loudly say, "Get down" as I moved very slowly to see who it was. At that moment, I was looking down the barrel of a large revolver pointed at someone else, the bartender. I was the only one who had not hit the ground, so I took off running out the bar around the corner to a buddy's apartment. He allowed me to use the bedroom where I lay delirious for hours watching the pictures and walls moving at odd paces. Death once again had knocked at my door. This would become a long, dark, and tedious 28-year journey filled with every evil spirit imaginable. The fear, bondage, whoredom and heaviness would at some point become a drag on my life and take its tow.

Adulthood: All Hell Breaks Loose

By my nineteenth birthday, I began to use heroin, a drug I'd sworn never to try. I was always leery of this drug because of how I'd witnessed its effects on others. To me, heroin represented sure death; it was taken intravenously, often times using dirty needles. I saw guys overdose only to be revived by a user buddy shooting salt water in their veins. I also witnessed a user die after his user buddies abandoned him. Heroin users "shot up" in their necks, penises; anywhere their veins were not burned out. The habit was classless; the users appeared totally hopeless. It did not take a genius to recognize a heroin addict; their behavior gave them away.

At the time, I still lived with Ma and her new husband. I had no problem paying the $200.00 she demanded for rent each month. Not contributing to a household was not an option for a grown Harris boy, so I worked hard at the mill. I was usually late and habitually high, but I went. My work ethic had become abysmal, and the men on the previous shift became angry at me for being late constantly.

They didn't know it, but I had fallen into the snares of the enemy and experimented with heroin. I believed that if I tried it just once, it wouldn't control me and I could quit if I didn't like it. I was strung out on heroin for at least a year. I purposely stayed away from others who used the drug to help myself get off it. I know now it was only by the grace of God that I was able to get through this time. When I would see my old heroin buddies, they attempted to draw me back into their web. But I chose the company of my regular alcohol and drugs of choice cause these were substances I thought I had control over. I never liked substances controlling me. There remnants of my year long heroin addiction was an ugly small needle track on my arm. Despite this habit, I was still able to pay Ma, save $150.00 in the credit union and keep three to four hundred for myself every two weeks.

After losing my job, I signed with a traveling sales magazine operation, which turned out to be a scam. One evening a few associates and I had prepared to go see James Brown in concert in downtown Baltimore, Maryland. We were in our hotel rooms getting ready, and getting high on red devils (downers) and sniffing airplane glue. I passed out and when I awoke in the room on the floor, the James Brown concert was over, my money was gone, and so was the traveling magazine operation. I once again dodged death, but this was the beginning of my reality being on my own.

I called Ma, and she and my sister came to get me. Believing she had groomed me enough to face the cruel world alone, she soon thereafter put me out. I felt she chose her husband over me. I didn't know God and had little understanding about God at that time. I kept working to supply my basic needs (shelter, food, and clothing) as well as feeding my addiction to cigarettes, pot and other habits. My new sport of choice became pool sharking. It was costly and time consuming to master but I did pretty well once I got it.

Between ages 18 and 40, I was in complete denial of my drug problem and unconscious of it as sin. I lacked God-consciousness in my life, thinking I was all right and the world was all wrong became acceptable to me. My only teachers were slicks, pimps, drug sellers, users and abusers, and thieves. No doubt, some of them were excellent teachers even though they taught wrong things. The majority of them handled mass dollars, drove Cadillac's, wore sharp shoes, clothes and fine jewelry. Being around this toxic element made it easy to hook up with these wilderness mentalities and con, scheme, and manipulate the system. By then I had been out on "World Avenue" for five years and had now enrolled in "Sin University."

At twenty-one, I met my first wife while emulating the pimps, hustlers, gangsters, and playboys I'd been hanging with. As I recall, we first met while I was standing on a street corner adjacent to the poolroom after just getting off my steel mill job. She pulled up and over and we began talking and later dating. Nineteen, fresh out of high school, athletic, a cheerleader, and from a respectable family, she would become my first love. We married soon after our first son was on the way. Dad had told me that if you make a baby, you should be responsible. I would later discover that I had a limited understanding of what it meant to be accountable and responsible.

I was cognizant and thankful I was not on heroin because a year before I got married, I faced a distressing experience. I was homeless for a few days before my auntie and her husband allowed me to live with them on the Eastside. In 1970 there was a major snow storm when 6 to 8 inches shut the entire town down. Not a vehicle was moving this early morning and I needed to get on the Southside, my turf, to get my hustle and heroin fix on. This was my first withdrawal experience and I was in a knot. I attempted to walk there which is normally a 30 to 45 minutes walk, but I was a lone soul out there. Conditions prohibited me from getting very far and I was forced back to Auntie's house. I went to my room shut the door and stayed in a fetal position for hours where I suffered through withdrawal.

After my son was born, I had my last encounter with heroin. I went outside for some air and headed toward an old friend's house. He was a minor pimp; his older brother was a major pimp who was our role model. I was attracted to the life being surrounded by women even though I did not like how pimps treated women. My friend's parents were Godly people whom I respected. After greeting them, I went back to his room where I found my friend shooting up. He asked me if I wanted some. I refused at first. I underestimated the power this temptation had over me. This was brown dope (heroin), the queen of the crop variety, and he was very high. I finally gave in, forgetting how much I hated the feeling and pain. I experienced my first and last overdose. Another brush with death, I felt life slipping away, my life was dissipating. Yet this time, it was not somebody else in a drug house or abandoned apartment. My friend brought me back, shooting salt water into my vein. I know today it was the Lord Jesus Christ who spared my life that day.

I had become a family man and needed to keep food on the table. I got another job at Republic Steel Mill in Warren, Ohio as a Tow Motor Operator making good money. I was laid off after six months after which my father-in-law got me a job with one of his friends who owned a vending machine operation. As head delivery and truck operator, I was responsible for the delivery truck, equipment, radio calls, and a two-man crew within an 80 miles radius. While the money was not nearly as good as my mill jobs, I had daily access to a myriad of bars, hotels, bowling alleys, and various clubs which carried the company's equipment. I enjoyed the freedom of the job and the perks that came along with it such as barmaids, beer, and good food. I worked the job for three and a half years--- drinking, driving, and working. I went to work faithfully, had no problems and was in control so I perceived. My machine repairmen taught me the fine art of drinking a shot and a beer like a man. I was in my glory. Not knowing the bondage I was in, I abused myself, my family, and those around me with my attitude.

Nearly twenty-two years old, my second son on the way and I still had not found a purpose for my life. Republic Steel called me back to work, but I turned them down preferring the decent benefits and a job that provided me a place to drink daily. There did come a day when I did give up the freedom of the Acme Music Vending Company job.

On June 1, 1974, my wife called during lunch hour to tell me the electric company had called me to schedule an interview the following day. My brother-in-law, who worked there, encouraged me to apply. I was reluctant to leave my current job after three and a half years because I was treated well and was my own boss. After the interviewing with the electric company the next morning, my decision became obvious. I was offered the opportunity for a free education to become a Tree trimmer with options lateral and horizontal. I was to make $3.88 per hour with a dollar yearly increase including family medical, dental, and other benefits. This job was too good to turn down. The opportunity for advancement and the job security was second to none. I was hired on June 4, 1974 and on my way to becoming accountable and responsible so I thought.

I started this job with a bad attitude and eventually got caught up in the prejudices and biases of union and company as it pertained to treatment and promotion of minorities. I began to hate, blame, and accuse white folks for my problems. Before that time, I had not gotten caught up in racial hatred and even had a few White and Hispanic friends from the neighborhood where I grew up.

Despite my lack of first-hand experience, I knew prejudice when confronted and when I observed it. I became a self-proclaimed discrimination lawyer, so to speak. I was one hundred percent supportive of the union, like my kindred, but after that everything was black versus white. Seven to eight months after I was hired, the company hired some white guys off the street and gave them seniority over the six of us previously hired. That was the first time I witnessed and experienced first-hand the mistreatment of blacks at the hands of whites.

Three years after beginning on the job and the birth of our third soon, I bought our first home. It was a beautiful brick two story with original French doors and glass with oak floors located in an older influential upper north side neighborhood. At this time, I was making a living but had no life. The more I worked, the more I made, and the more we spent. More and more, I wasn't at home spending time with my wife and sons. My attitude was that because I bought the house and paid the bills and mortgage, the rest was up to my wife. My only relief from work was more drinking and smoking (pot and cigarettes) and running my life the only way I knew how.

I did not have much of a relationship with my wife or with myself. I don't even remember how she felt or if she even cared that I wasn't around much. We seemed to talk at each other not to each other. I was unwilling to hear what she had to say. I had a "my way or the highway" mentality.

I did not believe I had an alcohol or drug problem. Furthermore, no one could have suggested otherwise because I wouldn't hear of it anyway.

I experienced some good times with my sons when they were growing up. My two oldest boys were playing little league football and baseball in the late 70's and early 80's. During those years, I would come home and the entire family would head for football and baseball practices. We were always on time. We met a diverse group of people along the way. Our sons' teams were very talented, winning three championships.

Making ends meet was hard even though I was making $10.88 an hour by 1980. I had a number of side jobs but lacked money management and budgeting skills. My then wife was equally inept; the checkbook was never correctly balanced.

Despite our financial challenges, in 1980, I took a vacation to Los Angeles, California to visit my baby brother and seek some peace. I was too selfish and self-absorbed to ever take my wife on vacation. I used trips as opportunities to isolate myself. After returning home after nearly two weeks, I could sense the high tension in the atmosphere. My wife and I got into another argument during which she said something derogatory towards my mother. In a fit of rage, I struck her across her face. At the time, I was wearing a cast on my hand which increased the impact of the blow.

My wife took our sons to her mother's house. I knew no other way to handle my wife's out- bursts, and what I believed to be disrespectful slanderous accusations, and her vile mouth. It was as if I was living the way my dad treated my ma. Though I was now in my early 30's, things in my life weren't getting better, they were getting worse.

During our separation and near our divorce, my mind entertained jealous spirits accompanied by homicidal thoughts. One night, I went to a bar to medicate my hurts and feelings. I was wearing a brand new $300 leather suit. I looked good on the outside, but on the inside I was desolate, all messed up and ready to detonate. When leaving the bar, I got it in my mind that my wife was at the home of the man she'd been sleeping with. My words are softer now, but surely were not nice at the time of this unpleasant incident. After making a brief appearance at a party, I devised a plan to catch her cheating. I wanted to show her that nobody disrespects my manhood and plays me for a fool. Noticing her car at his house, I turned my Cadillac around and parked it up the street out of sight of the boyfriend's home. By then it was about 4:00a.m. The thought of her having the nerve to park the car I purchased for her in his driveway added insult to the situation.

At around 6:00 a.m., I was still tipsy and grew tired of waiting for her to exit his home. She came out to go to work just as I anticipated. The false courage and bitterness which had been building rose to a boil. My anger escalated out of control; the hurt and pain that I felt she'd done to me overrode any thoughts of what I may have done to her. I had a pistol under my seat.

Not knowing which direction she would go, I waited as she started the car and backed up and headed in my direction. When she drove by, I expediently turned my car around. By the time she turned the corner,

I was next to her taunting her. I lowered my electric push window and demanded she pull over. She pulled off and I chased after her. At some point I began waving the pistol which intensified the chase. The chase continued for at least twenty city blocks until we reached a dead end. Infuriated, I got out and approached the car yelling, "Why did you cheat on me?" To my surprise, she denied cheating which raised my level of anger even more. I then grabbed her night bag out the back seat and ripped open to find a teddy and other fancy undergarments. Enraged, I demanded that she get out of her car into my car. We headed toward the nearby park where I continued to talk crazy. In the end, God did not allow me to physically harm her. I drove her back to her car where she was free to go. Today, I am so thankful that I didn't physically harm her. We have managed to remain friends today and are able to have healthy dialogue about our sons and grandchildren. It didn't happen overnight. For the next eleven years, the hate, hurt, and pain continued to fester. It was not until I turned forty-three years old, and was delivered from my sinful mindset that I developed a broken heart and contrite spirit which allowed the healing to begin.

Until then, I had no idea of what I had put my wife through. I didn't know myself nor did I know my wife. Today, I realize I was spiritually dead. I had life but wasn't living.

Walking in the Valley of Death

After the divorce in 1982, I was still psychologically traumatized and still addicted to drugs and alcohol. I wasn't then and still am not clear today, what led her to leave me for another man, who appearedto be worse off than me. Though I used and occasionally sold drugs, I never subjected my wife to that way of life. I was devastated, hurt, and close to a mental breakdown. The pain and memory caused by my dad leaving us resurfaced. On one hand, I hated my ex-wife and the so-called friends who knew about her affair but didn't tell me. I loved my wife, though it was selfish, self-centered and the worldly kind of love. It was the only love I knew. When this love didn't get its way, it fussed, cussed, clawed and acted mean. As always, I didn't know how to deal with these feelings except by using drugs and alcohol. I even considered suicide during this point in my life.

I continued to hang out in bars, "crying in my beer." I would then go home feeling sorry for myself. I sought solace with other recent divorcees. I even sought the counsel of my mom and dad, but to no avail because I wouldn't hear what they had to say. None of the advice I received soothed my agony, broken heartedness, and negative feelings. Not knowing Jesus, I had no one to trust with this problem but my dad. He was not empathetic to my needs. Besides he had his own difficulties and I was also reluctant to share my heartaches. I was forced to bear this heavy burden alone.

A year after the divorce, I was not any closer to healing. I do not recall experiencing happiness or sense of wholeness during this period in my life. The one event that I do recall from that year was going to a friend's house in Cleveland on August 13th, my birthday. We were getting high while preparing to go to a Rick James concert that evening. We drank and smoked cannabis and crack while listening to The group Funkadelic's music. Something told me to call home. When I did I received word my Dad had taken ill, and I should come home immediately.

I recall becoming faint, fearful, lightheaded, and bewildered. My eyes welled up with tears; immense sadness overwhelmed my heart as I raced down the 60 mile stretch of highway all alone. I returned to Dad's house and my auntie who lived across the street said "he's been taken to the hospital". Still trembling, I rushed to the hospital arriving in five minutes. When I approached his room, I passed by nurses, other hospital workers and other unfamiliar faces. When I walked in, Dad was strapped down to a bed. I was angered when I realized that no one was around him. He appeared trapped, squirming with a look of displeasure and disgust on his face. I'll never forget that look. I got even angrier.

Dad recognized me and said, **"This is a drag, son,"** a statement he often used when he was aggravated or disgusted. He then instructed me to go home and make sure everything in his house was secure. I don't recall Dad ever having been in the hospital. I didn't understand quite what was going on with my dad medically. I wanted to confer with my oldest sister and her family. No sooner than I arrived at his house to attend to his request before I stepped in, the phone rang. It was my auntie summoning me back to the hospital. I became even more nervous and afraid. When I got there, I was told that Dad had passed away. My feelings of abandonment, hatred and loneliness had never been more heightened. This was only the second time in my life that I had experienced death this close to me. The first time was when Granddaddy Henry, my dad's father died in 1977. I don't remember much about it except that I was among a long line of family members who traveled up the dim stairway and narrow hallway into my grandfather's room to say our goodbyes.

Back then, my dad was my god, and my god was dead. I trusted, believed, and depended on Dad even though our relationship was at times strained. I immediately began blaming the hospital, doctors, and nurses, and even my eldest sister. After all, it was she who had authorized the two surgeries within a four-hour period. It turned out that his appendix had ruptured, sending poison throughout his system. I felt my sister had taken Dad's life into her own hands not considering that he had never been in the hospital. She hadn't even consulted me in the process which irritated me and deepened my resentment.

These thoughts plagued me up to the time of Dad's burial. I questioned what had led to my father's demise, but no one seemed to understand, not even my ma. Most of my friends didn't know what it felt like to lose a father. I remember asking a God I did not know why this had happened. Today, I look to God and ask, "Why not me?"

My father's death resulted in my many mood changes drastically and led to what would be by far the most evil year of my thirty-three years. Dad's death led me into a personal perpetual downward spiral in my life. As was my pattern, I drank and smoked to mask the pain. This time, I did so at an increased pace and often did so alone. Drinking was already a part of the tradition of death. Relatives, extended family and friends sat around before, during and after the burial drinking while sharing various stories of my dad. Someone like me, with an alcohol problem, had an acceptable space and time to indulge the habit. Dad had keep an assortment of half gallon top shelf liquors stashed away for his company or entertainment purposes. I drank profusely and formulated my own little isolated world inside his house.

Though I was totally lost, scared, and helpless, and felt like crying, my goal was to not let anyone see me breakdown. I didn't want anyone to see me as weak or vulnerable. I accepted the lyrics of the old Temptations song that "A Man Ain't Supposed To Cry." I bottled all my tears until I was all alone at night.

After Dad's departure, I began traveling down new roads of self-destructive behavior. Roads I would not wish on anyone. After we buried Dad, I took off the dark rose-colored sunglasses that covered my teary blood shot swollen eyes. All hell was about to erupt. It began with the disappearance of his will.

While Dad's lady friend and I had witnessed his will, when family members went to Dad's safety deposit box to retrieve it, the will was somehow missing. Another friend of my dads confirmed she had assisted in writing the will. The will directed that I live in his home. I searched his personal written documents daily to see if I could find it, to no avail. I was unaware he had placed it in his safety deposit box at his bank. As I unpacked divorce papers, union business, home buying transactions, and a host of other important documents, I was reminded of the many chaotic times dad and our family had lived through. I also lost trust in my auntie and others. Whether my recollection of there being a will is correct or not,

I felt that as the oldest son, I should have been responsible for my father's estate. In all truthfulness, I was in no condition to handle Dad's business. Nevertheless, I grew bitter towards my sister. I felt all my brothers and sisters should have been involved in handing Dad's affairs. Dad loved us all without favoritism. Who gave certain people this authority to check his safety deposit box? Who gave anyone the right to distribute Dad's possessions to whomever they desired? My bitterness reached a pinnacle and caused a rift in my sibling relationship.

On one occasion, while meeting at the attorney's office, my sister and I started arguing and I called her a bitch. That was totally out of character for me, and was the first time I'd called my sister out of her name. As a result, our relationship was severed. My baby brother came in town to receive his share of the estate and my dad's car and quickly departed. I wanted my dad's home, but my sister wasn't open to it. I had heard of these type family squabbles after death, and was being confronted with it personally. Surprisingly, dad had left $77,000 among the six children. In addition to feeling like I was slighted by my sister being in control of my dad's estate, I was fresh from my divorce, drinking like a sieve, and drugging hard core. My ten years of hell was just beginning.

Despite the chaos in my life, I was still holding down a job. When my father died, my company gave me three days of paid leave. Drinking and drugging continued to be my way of life, a coping mechanism, the way I handled loss. When I wasn't working, I was using.

A drug dealer friend advised me to never ever try crack cocaine. I had heard about Richard Pryor's crack episode (including when he set himself on fire). Though I had snorted plenty of powder cocaine, I had never experienced or been interested in using crack cocaine. After my dad's death, that changed. Not long after burying Dad and before getting my inheritance, I explored crack with a friend after coming home from a bar. It only took that one time to put me in crack bondage for the next ten years of my life (August 1983 to September 1993). I was still too macho, arrogant and strong-willed to admit I had a drug problem. Crack became my drug of choice to deal with my negative emotions. Crack-dependent, I maintained my course of self-destruction, hurting people, stepping on others and being extremely rebellious. I was trapped by the snares of evil running from bar to bar, woman to woman and drug dealer to drug dealer.

I experienced another loss again overwhelmed, this time Ma's mother. Gran-ma was a woman of God, beautiful in body and spirit, and an excellent professional cook and baker. She died on February 7, 1984, not long after my dad and in the middle of my new found crack habit.

In 1985, I wanted some stability, so I decided to marry again. Marriage, I thought, would heal my loneliness and feelings of abandonment. I wanted someone that understood me, my hurts and needs. I met a twenty-four year old woman, I was ten years older. She met all my sexual needs, which was good enough for me. I thought I could grow to love her. I did, and still do today unconditionally. But once again, I did not know myself, my wife, or her family because of my self-centered and selfishness. I didn't care about anything but my own wants and needs. I was determined to get them met, come hell or high water.

She knew of my drug use and even engaged in drinking and snorting with me. But I felt responsiblefor introducing her to crack cocaine, which I still regret today. We had two handsome sons in the first two years and a daughter the following year. Despite our drug use, all of our children were born healthy. I was overwhelmed with the responsibility of family as well as a wife whom I did not trust. We lived in an environment that was unhealthy, both because of substance abuse and poor communication. It was within this environment that I experienced another tremendous loss.

In 1987, I received a truck radio message telling me to come back to the shop. When I got there, I received the devastating news that my mother had passed away. She'd been suffering with skin cancer for the last eight years, including chemotherapy treatments and excessive pains. Until I got the call, I thought I had prepared myself for her death. Feelings of abandonment, loneliness, and pain had erupted once again. I didn't know how to handle the fact that someone that was so dear to me was gone.

I began recalling other losses, including my first divorce. The fact that my first wife kept my dog, a German shepherd, named Toby. He was a pedigree, dark black with streaks of white running from his chest to his neck. We had graduated from eight weeks of dog obedience school; he stood high and proud. Months after the divorce, this dog I loved died. I had never grieved his death until now. My mother's death was yet another loss I was not able to handle.

I understand now that Ma had gone home to be with the Lord. I remember vividly the last days of her life. She was no longer cussing in her latter days and the pain appeared to subside. She had peaceful facial expressions and her tone of voice had softened. The day before she died, she sent me to get one of her favorite fast food meals. When I returned to the hospital she had no desire to eat or talk and asked that we let her rest. Today, I believe through faith I'll see her again one day and that thought brings tears of joy to my heart and soul. I thank God for the promise of that reunion.

When the family got together to bury Ma, I had no desire to be involved. These losses deepened my bitterness and my inability to show love. The downward spiral of my life continued out of control. I was miserable, so I wanted everyone around me to be also including my wife, family and friends. I did not realize that these were the workings of the enemy. I had no power to stop the pattern despite my good intentions. When Ma died, I was without anyone to turn to in time of trouble and need. I began to think about how I would take all the knowledge and things Ma and Dad taught me and make the best of it. I was forced to grow up all alone because I did not know Jesus.

At thirty-seven, I had never known true peace, happiness, love, responsibility, contentment, joy, or wholeness. I was, however, becoming conscious of the void in my life, avoid which grew larger. The negative emotions I'd carried so many years had hardened my heart. I was not in tune to the Gospel of Jesus Christ. I did not know scripture and lacked all spiritual knowledge. I was truly separated from God.

As the years rolled on, my life got no better. I had no peace, inwardly or outwardly. Everything around me seemed to exasperate my negative emotions. Darkness had dominion over my life and my thoughts. I had no idea where my life or family was headed. I had no one to love or trust with my painful realities. Besides that, I didn't want anyone to know that I was stuck in the "miry clay."

A back injury I'd sustained in 1985 recurred in 1991, putting me out of work for about six months. Though I collected benefits, responsibilities and burdens of marriage and family as well as my addiction continued to weigh me down. My ability to cope with life's terms was virtually non-existent. The only way I knew how to cope was by getting high.

I didn't have a good relationship with my wife or my ex-wife as well as my older sister. My life had no meaning or purpose. I hadn't learned how to be a good dad, husband or man. I persisted on engaging in self-destructive behavior and remaining in bondage to substances I had no control over, and in which truthfully, I did not care to indulge. It was only by the grace of God that I did not die from engaging and using drugs. I thank the Lord for that! The only thing that I did consistently well was work, but now the company was threatening to stop my benefits and possibly terminate me. I believed these threats were due in part to discriminatory and anti-union factors.

In addition to not being back at work, my wife and I were discussing separation. I was depressed: a walking time bomb. My company's treatment added to the stress and vengeful anger I was feeling. At that point, I knew I needed help so I visited a psychiatrist who diagnosed me as being manic depressive. He prescribed me some valium and sent me on my way. I had used valium in the 1960s, but I had graduated from valium years before. I didn't need another downer, so I decided to sell them on the street. Feeling hopeless and suicidal, I was determined to use my own power to shake myself out.

Everything in life was crumbling before me—my job, my family—everything. There seemed to be no evidence of hope around me. I had been on crack for eight years and could finally admit to having a problem which I was powerless to stop. I hated every minute and every hit of cocaine. I now comprehended the ways that it destroyed my life, family, and the smidgen of sanity I had left. So, I covertly entered a rehabilitation facility, without enlisting my wife's support. Admitting my addiction and getting help for it, left me feeling like less of a man, father, husband. I felt like a socially unacceptable citizen.

I entered a facility as an in-patient for 30 days. My treatment included attending meetings to disclose some of my shortcomings and character defects. Admitting I was an addict and hanging out with others like me was normal. But for the first time in life, I started reading God's word consistently. I felt a tugging at my heart from a power greater than me. Turning to God's word was the last resort for me; my options had decreased. Eight scriptures became ingrained in my heart during this time:

"Casting all your care upon him; for hecareth for you. " (1 Peter 5:7 KJV).

Come unto me, all ye that labour and are heavy laden, and I will give you rest."(Matthew 11:28 KJV).

But seek ye first the kingdom of God, and his righteousness; and all these things shall be added unto you. (Matthew 6:33 KJV).

God has said, "I will never forsake thee, nor forsake thee." (Hebrews 13:5 KJV).

Wherefore, if any man be in Christ, he is a new creature: old things are passed away; behold, all things are become new."(2 Corinthians 5:17 KJV).

And we know that in all things God work together for good to them that love God, to them who are the called according to His purpose.(Romans 8:28 KJV).

What shall we then say to these things? If God be for us, who can be against us? (Romans 8:31 KJV).

For if ye forgive men their trespasses, your heavenly Father will also forgive you. (Matthew 6:14 KJV).

"I can do all things through Christ which strengtheneth me. (Philippians.4:13 KJV).

Although I had not yet been saved from my sins, I did begin seeking God in my life. I did meet God in the rooms or the meetings, but it is possible to meet the omnipresent God anywhere. Despite my growing relationship with God, I was still a walking time bomb which could discharge at any time. This became especially clear after my first thirty days in rehab. My recovery process was marred by my marital and family problems.

After earning a home pass, I walked home without calling home first. Besides, our home phone was turned off, so the only way I could have called was to call my auntie who lived across the street. For the most part, I enjoyed the 30 minute walk home, though I felt some guilt about my being absent and not supporting my family. Since I was sober, my mind was processing and attempting to differentiate feelings I used to cover-up with substances. But I was still in prison mentally mode, prison in which I stayed for years to come.

When I approached my home during one visit, my wife was on the porch appearing to be engaged in a jovial conversation with a man. Feeling jealous, I recommended that he leave and never be caught on my property. He left. After arguing, my wife who I thought was lying about her relationship with this man, I spoke to my children and then I left.

Duringthe seemingly long walk back to the facility, my thoughts and feelings were racing. I was determined to finish the recovery process for my own self preservation and dignity. I wanted to become a better person. I finished the voluntary 90-day rehabilitation program which was difficult. During that time, I learned how to disclose pain and grief especially with regard to my parents. I fasted for the first time, read my bible passionately, and wrote down scriptures as my heart was pricked. I was diligently seeking this Jesus I was reading about.

Even though my worries had not ceased, I knew God was embedding his word in my heart. When I went back home, my newly found sober lifestyle was not congruent with the home environment to which I returned. I enjoyed the new feeling of being sober. I was 88 days drug free and experiencing my release from hell on earth, yet distrust and lack of communication between my wife and me continued. It only took me a couple of days to realize she only knew the old Richard. My wife didn't understand the concept of sobriety and didn't want to address her own issues. My discussions with her were all for naught.

While she occupied our bed night after night, I would sit angrily in the living room watching and reading pornography. My wife was not meeting my sexual desires which I thought she owed me. To me, the woman's purpose was to satisfy her husband. The desire to get my sexual needs met led me to leave my wife and move in with another woman. While I wanted my wife, I wanted to get revenge for her indiscretions, make her jealous and truthfully show her that I still had game. I blamed her for a lot of my inadequacies, pain, misery and issues. I looked okay from outer appearances, but inside I was hurting for certain.

Trying to come off drugs and alcohol was made more difficult by my love of money. After returning home, I remember receiving $13,000, one of three sums I received. I used this sum to buy a living room set, bedroom set, and to pay a variety of long overdue bills, including rent. I also bought a car at an auction for $850.00. I gave my wife a few hundred dollars. The rest was spent on drugs and alcohol to feed my wife's and my addiction.

In Solitary Confinement to the Power of Sin and Death

We know that the law is spiritual; but I am carnal, sold under sin. For that which I do I allow not: for what I would, that do I not; but what I hate, that do I. If then I do that which I would not, I consent unto the law that it is good. Now then it is no more I that do it, but sin that dwelleth in me. For I know that in me (that is, in my flesh) dwelleth no good thing: For to will is present with me; but how to perform that which is good I find not. For the good that I would I do not: but the evil which I would not, that I do. Now if I do that I would not, it is no more I that do it, but sin that dwelleth in me, O wretched man that I am. Who shall deliver me from the body of this death? I thank God through Jesus Christ our Lord. (Romans 7:14-20, 24, 25 KJV)

I am not blaming nor accusing my wife for my own failings; I am merely indicating where my rehabilitation and our marriage were headed. She was disinterested in going to counseling, meetings, or any other programs that would help us sober up and heal. I knew I was losing her, when deep down I needed encouragement from her. I remembered part of a scripture Paul wrote "If God be for us, who can be against us?" (Romans 8:31 KJV) I needed someone for me not against me. But I continued to look for that in other people, instead of Jesus Christ. The breakdown of our marriage combined with my wife's father's hospitalization for his diabetic condition only made matters worse. Subsequently, he died on my 105 day of sobriety. I had yet to experience anyone's death while sober. I struggled trying to conceptualize what she was going through as well as discerning my own emotions. I wanted to be there for her, but was also concerned about my new quality of life.

I had been cautioned in rehab about returning to the same people, places, and things that might get in the way of my sobriety. However, I had not yet changed my tough, stubborn, and rebellious attitude. I continued to engage in addictive and erratic thinking during this process. I had been sober for a little over three months. As a result, my perception was a little clearer which made it more difficult for anyone to manipulate, con, or lie to me. I was not of the same mindset. Rather, I was seeking a different quality of well being.

The situation the day before the funeral tested my newfound discernment. My children and I were spending time at my wife's mother's house. She had left with out- of-town relatives earlier that morning. The children and I had remained at her mom's house for approximately six hours. At some point, I became concerned about my wife's whereabouts and activities. Our house was nearby so I decided to leave the children to check to see if my suspicion was true. As I approached our home, I noticed the relative's car and knew in my gut that something wasn't right. As I cautiously opened the door, I was absolutely taken aback to find my wife and others using drugs. I would not tolerate this disrespect in my house, I felt as if I had used myself. Angry, I warned them if they did not leave my residence immediately I would call the police. I then proceeded back to her mother's house feeling irate and violated. Old emotions and "stinking thinking" began to bubble up. I was a nervous wreck the rest of the evening feeling alone and apprehensive about the future. I had been on a tedious crack cocaine journey since 1983. While I had emerged out of the hell hole, I was now facing another dilemma about whether I would return to drugs.

Later that night, I became extremely restless and agitated. My wife was still out doing her thing, and I had become jealous and furious. I had no phone at home to call my human sponsor and it was past 2:30 a.m. To my surprise, I dropped to my knees to pray to God about my pain. The next few days I attended extra meetings and talked to my sponsor. The things my sponsor said sounded good, but my mind was clouded. I felt like I had used even though I hadn't. My mind returned to the state of user mentality and I did not know where to turn, except to the place that was already so familiar. I fell back into the trap. I felt deceived by Satan, my wife, and the rehab system that convinced me to trust in human sponsors. I reverted back to hell on earth---body, soul, and mind. I returned to my addiction. Distraught, regretful, and sorrowful for relapsing I hated myself, life, and surroundings. I knew this hell was real and I truly did not want to be a participant. The acknowledgement that my life was a living hell added to my woe. Crack had taken me back to a hell which was even hotter and tormenting than before. Thanks be to God, I only went half way back into the pit, knowing that every drink, hit of crack, and drug brought pure misery. Though I was cognizant of the suffering and pain that would come I was tired, my foolish state of mind caused me to continue my old ways. I had read enough Good News to know that being disobedient to God contributed to my pain and misery.

This would be the last Christmas with my wife and kids. Knowing this caused a daily struggle. I didn't know that Jesus was the reason for the season, so my holidays were always full of materialistic, selfless, and commercial possessions. I had been deceived into a worldview that was devoid of God. My worldly wisdom, substance abuse, and sin contributed to my depression, oppression, and attitude. I was walking around spiritually dead. As James conveys, "For as the body without the spirit is dead." (James 2:26 KJV)

The amount of loneliness, emotional stress and pain, I experienced in 1992 was similar to what I had experienced in 1991. The year 1992 brought a host of uncertainties, unemployment and a torn family among other things. Similar to my first marriage, I felt the foundation of my family crumbling before me. Though I still had not developed a personal relationship with Jesus I remembered parts of scriptures which resonated with my circumstances. *"Except the Lord build the house, they labor in vain"* (Psalm 127: 1 KJV) and *"And everyone that heareth these sayings of mine, and doeth them not, shall be likened unto a foolish man, which built his house upon the sand." (Matthew 7:26 KJV)* rang true as I reflected back on my life, I was wallowing in and not walking through the Valley of the Shadow of Death. I lay wallowing not walking through. I attributed luck to anything good that happened in my life, never thanking God or anyone else for my successes. On the rare occasions, I would drop to my knees and pray for God to lift a burden or problem, seconds afterwards I would forget God. Even after the innumerable blessings given me daily, my concern was what I had, could get, and what's in it for me. I was a poor example of a husband, father, and a man. I believed in beating the system that was beating me. They owed me. I never understood how I could be married but also lonely. How I could never satisfy my sexual desires. How I could never feel whole or appreciated. I wanted to be loved and valued but did not know how to love or value others. My heart was full of resentment. The only emotion I was able to show was anger. I couldn't give or receive love. On the days when I woke up feeling good, I would blow it by getting high.

While I was seeking God more fervently at this stage of my life, my choices did not reflect so. Satan's voice rang louder in my ear. After all, I had been walking with Satan for over 25 years. My heart remained 100% loyal and dedicated to him. I didn't realize that my purpose in life was to live for Jesus. Today, I can reflect back on my life and say, "Thank you Jesus God for everything."

Back then, I didn't like myself or others. I would not let others in my world nor did I want to enter in theirs. I found myself on an island desolate, withdrawn, and isolated. There were burdens on my heart too heavy for me to bear. I had a weight on my shoulders I could no longer carry. The mask I wore for years began to crumble. My fake "everything's ok" smile turned to gloom. For the longest time, I wondered where my authentic smile went. Now I realized the Devil had stolen it from me along with my complete identity.

My friends and family faded away, I had either chased them away or they left willingly. For whatever reason, they were gone. My brother, Mike, took his family and moved to Arizona. My baby brother lived in Los Angeles. Relatives who were close in proximity became emotionally distant. I was on an island, all alone, up to my nose in quicksand. I was lost.

There was one person who stood by me during this time, my doctor who constantly came to my rescue encouraging, trusting, and accepting me into his home. I loved him as a person, a father, and a professional. Though I let him down, he never forsook me. He helped me survive my first Thanksgiving and Christmas without my family. In my lowest state, he was there in every aspect. I wanted for nothing materially. Later, I recognized that the love, mercy and humility of this man were the attributes of Jesus.

The year 1993 was both a beginning and an ending. Specifically, it was my last year on crack cocaine. The discrimination lawsuit against my employer was settled, another victory. Now I would get through this year by entering another pit of despair. I blew the money from the lawsuit with riotous living. This left me broke and tired. After that, I experienced

45

several losses. My paternal grandmother passed away suddenly. Her death along with being separated from my wife and children, drug use and the job loss caused much anguish. I did odd jobs to help support me and my habit.

I was still a narrow minded thinker who did things my way and allowed pride and foolishness to keep me stuck in the muck and mire. Adding to that was the loss of my maternal grandpa. This loss caused me to begin calculating the number of family members I'd lost over the last ten years. I was frightened and began to have suicidal thoughts. In mid-1993, one day I decided to take a long lunch break from a private landscaping job. It was not uncommon for me to have a beer with lunch, but this particular day I stopped and purchased crack for later. On my way there, I was bewildered to see my wife and kids being driven around by the guy whom I had seen at my home during my rehabilitation. I became enraged by them both, him for deliberately disrespect, and her for blatantly lying to me. My mindset said "you don't allow anyone to take what is rightfully yours." I acted in accordance with my mind set. Even though my wife and I were separated, it appeared to me that she and this guy were flaunting their relationship. My children being with her made me even angrier. This was also forcing me to face the reality that there was little if any chance of my marriage getting back together. I was about to spin into a jealous rage. I wasn't concerned about what I may have put her through; I only cared about what I was going through.

I was not motivated by love for my family as much as I was motivated by jealousy and the desire to seek revenge. "Hurt people hurt people" is a saying I had heard in recovery. Still unconsciously hurt from my mom leaving my dad, first marriage, and the hurt of my second wife leaving me was overpowering. Despite all my emotions, I was somehow able to keep myself from confronting them that day.

As the next week began, I ran into my wife and her "boyfriend" on various occasions in different locations. The cat was now out the bag. I felt as if they were trying to "play me." The anger I repressed was turned toward drugs and alcohol. I vowed that if I saw them one more time, all hell was going to break loose. Continuing to cry in alcohol and drugs, in some distant part of my mind, I knew that doing something violent would lead to jail, death, or insanity. But I had no power to redirect my thoughts or feelings because I was deep in sin and the snares of evil. I began having gangster thoughts and wanted to hurt somebody and control something. I even thought about moving, leaving the city and joining the cartel. By this stage of my life, I had been engaged in a few gun battles and couriered some drugs and had developed an "I don't care" attitude; but I was not a killer. I did not want to hurt or harm anyone, but I could not let them hurt me either. I had been suffering too long and was too tired. Admittedly, I was still interacting with my wife which gave me some satisfaction. I could not lure her back because her family, friend and boyfriend didn't want her around me, but money and drugs were the perfect trap, and it worked every time. I knew she was still messing around with a drug dealer and drugs, so drugs was my way of getting back at her for being unfaithful. After all, she was still my wife.

By the end of April, 1993, I had started receiving Social Security checks, bought myself another car, and replenished my wardrobe. But I was still miserable and continued to put my life in dangerous situations. At this point, things finally came to a head with my wife and her boyfriend. I spotted them for the third time riding around seeming to throw their relationship in my face. On that particular day, I had left work on a major job, and was headed back to town to buy drugs and check on my wife and her boyfriend. I bought some beer and crack for later that evening and set out riding. I ran smack into my wife's boyfriend and her, and had the thought of scaring them. So I borrowed my young dope boy's model 9 millimeter pistol (which I had never shoot before) and unloaded it down the long narrow driveway of her mother's house at his car where he took refuge. Immediately after shooting nine shots, I went to a user associate's home where I prayed that I did not kill anyone. I spent the entire night getting high and getting information via phone and runner associates about my wife's boyfriend's condition. I learned that a single bullet ricocheted off the driveway pavement and scratched his ankle resulting in a superficial wound. His wound was bandaged and he'd been released.

Today, what I now realize was the voice of the enemy told me to take care of business and not to allow anyone to take anything else from me. At this point, I still didn't realize I had a jealous spirit, which was an evil spirit from the devil's hand. It wasn't until a year later, after I was incarcerated and studied the bible's account of Cain and Abel that I knew what was really in my heart. Jealousy ran in my family. I Thank God "But as for you, ye thought evil against me; but God meant it unto good, to bring to pass, as it is this day, to save much people alive."(Genesis 50:20 KJV).

I was later arrested and charged for the crime. I had a court appearance around early June after which my case was bound over to the grand jury. I was let out on bond. Since this was my first major brush with the law, I hired a lawyer and continued living the same insane way I had been. While I had many associates who had been in the criminal justice system, I'd never been caught for any of the dirt I had done. While I had not forgotten that I'd shot this character a couple of months earlier, I did return to life as usual—getting high and making poor decisions as a result.

I moved about the city all by myself, continuing in my mess. One day, I had just bought some drugs and settled in my new apartment which so happened was near where my wife and her boyfriend resided. I was getting high, paranoid, and lonely and confused about my life's experiences walking around the apartment noticing my shadow on the wall; when suddenly I heard two bullets and noticed they'd hit the hallway wall. When I realized that they were stray bullets actually being fired at me, I hit the floor. After about five minutes of no shots being heard, I crawled towards the living room window to peek out to see what was going on. I saw a car, but because it was dark, I couldn't figure out whose it was.

Assuming that my wife and her boyfriend were the culprits and I had again had a brush with death. I called my wife and threatened to produce an oozy and other street warfare gear. It was game on now. I continued to play war and mind games. As I did so, I sank deeper in quicksand. On top of that I received a phone call; my baby brother had been murdered, gunned down (which confirmed a vision I'd been shown months earlier).

My brother's murder triggered all the negative feelings imaginable, including guilt and shame. While I raised my brother, I could not save him from drugs and sin. I felt that I had molded him into the person he was, a slave to sin and drugs. My brother was truly gifted, athletic, and a good dad when not indulging in drugs. I couldn't save myself; I certainly couldn't save my brother. I was a complete failure. This time thinking my failure had resulted in the loss of yet another loved one.

I had nowhere to turn when my brother died. I didn't feel I could go on. I tried to reach my middle brother, but he was far out of town. This left a bad taste in my life; I felt like he had written off the family. The other relatives and friends appeared unconcerned. I guess they had written him off too since he was an addict. They had treated me likewise, but because of my addiction I could not control the stealing, lying, and manipulating and other behaviors which had alienated me from my family.

There was some dissent among the family and my brother's girlfriend as to whether or not my brother would be cremated. Cremation seemed out of order and disrespectful for my brother. Thank God, I was able to assist significantly financially which allowed him to be buried.

As with other adversities, I dealt with the pain, hate, bitterness, and resentment by using drugs and alcohol. Using had usually worked for me. But there was something about seeing my brother laying there that drugs and alcohol could not seem to numb. When I saw the bullet wound to his face, I stormed out of the funeral home. I was bitter and ready to kill. Who would I kill first? Should I take the law into my own hands? I took off in my car angry, confused, and extremely hurt, and hating the fact that I could actually feel it all. I remember driving very fast having no clue what to do or where to go, so I went to my apartment and had my own pity party. Somehow I got through the funeral; we all did without expressing any of our true feelings. We were a family who held secrets and feelings. During the whole ordeal, nobody asked me about how I was doing or feeling. I got questions about how he'd died, whether I had found out who did it, and if I was going to kill the person. This had been a pattern at all of the family funerals; no one was concerned about how I was feeling.

Over the next two months, I began to disassociate myself from phony people while waddling in the muck and mire and returning to the vomit that was my life. In early December, I got into a conflict with some youngsters over a gun. They jumped me but, I fought the three of them like the stark raving mad man I was. I found a pointed coal shovel in the area of the incident to use as a weapon. I swung that shovel with super strength and authority. I was under attack; it was a matter of life or death. I felt violated and enraged and in fear of someone taking something from me. I managed to make my break, landing on the neighbor's porch and jumping through their picture window. The youngsters then fled down the street and out of sight. Before dealing with my own injuries, I went to speak with the landlord about the broken window. I then admitted myself to the local hospital where I stayed the next three or four days. I was fixated on seeking revenge on the three culprits. In my way of thinking, I'd been on this earth too long to have kids jumping me. After all, I had sons their age and older. Furthermore, I wasn't going to allow anybody to put their hands on me. That's not how I rolled. I took pride in and even enjoyed being crazy and quick-tempered. I later learned that this mindset was nothing more than a defense mechanism to keep unwanted people out of my space.

During my second or third day in the hospital, I sat up in my bed contemplating my plan of revenge against the boys who had injured me and my ego. I looked out into the hospital hallway and noticed a familiar face, which turned out to be my cousin on my ma's side (my grandad and his dad were brothers).

My cousin and I had a lot in common. We were both baby boomers, had good jobs, wives, children and street mentalities with an addiction for sin. As he approached the entrance of my room, I observed a glowing and radiant countenance about him. I remembered a scripture I had read in rehab. "They looked unto him, and were lightened: and their faces were not ashamed." (Psalm 34:5 KJV). Cousin looked different. He looked good; his disposition and smile were genuine. His mere presence comforted me. He began witnessing and sharing the love of Jesus and how He had changed his life. He talked about how Jesus died for our sin, hang-ups and shortcomings, how Jesus forgave our sins, how the guilt and shame of our sins could be no more. He talked about how Jesus would never leave or forsake us and how we "should not be conformed to this world but transformed with the renewing of our minds." I had read about this same Jesus in the bible while in the rehab facility but had not seen or been witnessed to with such conviction. Then he asked me was I saved and did I have a personal relationship with the one and only true God. I thought about the question for a moment and answered no.

At that moment, I hoped to attain what my cousin had. We were on World Ave. together we both attended Sin University, and had serious substance issues. Little did I know, I would also join him in the journey through the "sin den" (prison) shortly thereafter. The thing that most amazed me about what he said was that Jesus was not a respecter of person's and, that I was eligible for this salvation and deliverance. If God could change and bring reconciliation to someone bound in sin like him, I believed I could have that personal relationship. That very moment, that very day, I accepted Jesus as my personal Lord and Savior.

I left the hospital forgetting all about the revenge I had in my heart when I went in. Strangely, I only wanted to go to church to find this Jesus my cousin had described. Though I was somewhat reluctant, the thought of how my cousin looked, his character radiated love, joy, and peace was something I longed for.

I went to church two times after my release from the hospital before January. My second time in church, Pastor Jenkins preached the message where he testified that he had also been lost and where Jesus brought him from. As he was speaking, I felt in my heart that what I was hearing was real, and that it was the only way out of the deep pit I had fallen into. Right then and there, I stood up and in accordance with Romans 10:9 That if thou shalt confess with my mouth the Lord Jesus, and believe in thine heart that God hath raised him from the dead". The difference between being at church was that I received the Holy Ghost and literally felt a transformation. January 2, 1994, my born again spiritual birthday, will be a special day for the rest of my life.

While January 2, 1994 marked the time that I was saved, filled with the Holy Ghost and delivered from self, my mind was not yet removed I was beginning to understand renewing my mind was going to be a life-long process. Life would continue to be arduous because I was a new born babe in Christ who had been a sinner for forty-three years. To help with my new walk, I joined the church that day and was given a spiritual advisor by Pastor Jenkins named Pastor McDowell. Pastor McDowell was an older gentleman. I was captivated by his biblical knowledge, understanding, and wisdom. I also liked the fact that he was a serious, no nonsense Christian who backed everything up by scripture. In his living room and basement office libraries were a wealth of scholarly, texts, bibles, concordances, and books. I felt extremely comfortable with him as a mentor. My new awareness of Jesus and learning biblical accounts captured my interest and expanded my mind. But I still lived in a world that did not support my new walk.

I was living with my brother's fiancée and my nephew during this time. She had a large apartment and only charged me $150.00 a month, so it was a good deal for me financially. I had a very large room to myself and bought my own food. The neighborhood was uptown and nice with all the conveniences I needed including bank, stores, and restaurants. I would pay rent, buy groceries, keep some pocket money, and put one thousand dollars in the bank monthly.

At the end of January, I was drug and cigarette free. But then the familiar voice beckoned me to get some money out of the bank and get high. I did not want to get high; I wanted to get free. But I was surrounded by drugs daily, both in the neighborhood and in my brother's fiancée's apartment. In fact, she used daily. I was hard pressed on every side; it was a very trying experience. I was helped tremendously by a church member I called Sister Jones. She'd given me, *"No weapon that is formed against thee shall prosper; and every tongue that shall rise against thee in judgment thou shall condemn. This is the heritage of the servants of the Lord, and their righteousness is of me, saith the Lord"* (Isaiah 54:17 KJV). I would speak these scriptures often as well as others like, *"If God be for us, who can* be against us?" (Romans8:31 KJV), "I can do all things through Christ which strengtheneth me! (Philippians 4:13 KJV) and "But seek ye first the kingdom of God, and His righteousness and all these things shall be added unto you." (Matthew6:33 KJV).

One day, I went to the bank to withdraw some money to get high. I cried and again felt rejected, lonely, and afraid to look up to God. I sat on the couch in the apartment having done what I did not want to do, feeling somewhat perplexed. As I was about to enter into a depressed mode, I looked out the picture window only to see my cousin pulling up. The still soft voice I was getting accustomed to, listening to, advised me to tell him the truth. The voice let me know that it was he who sent someone to confess my sin and shame. Something in my spirit nudged me to put down the pride and no longer hide it as I had done when sin consumed me. I thank God for sending him, since I had only been saved and delivered a little over a month and was still too weak to overcome this monstrous defeat alone. As I disclosed my backsliding incident, which was not easy, I saw the disappointment on my cousin's face. I even felt troubled that my actions might trigger him to regress. His facial expression and mood became flat which was tantamount to one who had just used. My cousin suggested we visit my spiritual advisor. The last thing I wanted to do was face Pastor McDowell. I already felt low, and knew that Pastor McDowell would chastise me. I did understand what it meant to "trust in the Lord with all thine heart; and lean not unto thine own understanding." (Proverbs 3:5 KJV) I was ignorant about what it meant to be guided and directed by God. But my options were limited. If there was any hope of getting back to Jesus and sobriety, I needed to make every possible effort.

I had to give this Jesus, salvation, and deliverance thing a valiant effort, just like I gave Satan for so many years.

When we arrived at his house, Pastor was sweeping his driveway so the meeting resembled a prodigal son coming home to open arms. Thinking I had already messed up with Jesus and now with this man, I was afraid to approach my spiritual coach. To my surprise, instead of scolding me, he welcomed me with open arms. I felt a relief like I had never felt before. After my cousin left, Pastor and I proceeded to his basement office. There we talked and I did as the scripture says, "confessed my faults one to another and, pray for one another, that ye may be healed" (James 5:16a KJV). This was a significant step in my spiritual growth because I learned the need for spiritual fellowship and laboring in Christ. I had already asked God to forgive me. *"If we confess our sins, He is faithful and just to forgive us our sins, and cleanse us from all unrighteousness."* (1John 1:9 KJV). But my ease only came after talking, praying, and being ministered to by Pastor McDowell. Pastor said one thing which really disturbed me during our talk. "You do not love Jesus because if you did…" he then took me directly to *John 14:15 KJV, "If you love me, keep my commandments."* That hurt because in my heart I truly did love Jesus. I also discussed how I always worked and had money and cigarettes, drugs, and sin were everyday occurrences. He said he noticed how my lifestyle appeared fine without money but as soon as I got money, I got high. He was right on, that's all I've ever done. He ministered to me about money and when he finished ministering God's word, he prophesied I would never do drugs again and that I'd be able to keep money in my pockets. I left feeling relieved and confident that

God could and would delivery me from the bondage of money. After that meeting, I never got high again.

On March 28, 1994, I wentto court to be tried for the charges arising from the incident with my wife and her boyfriend. The trial lasted two days. The Lord, Holy Spirit, and my eldest son were the only ones with me. I did not take the stand because I refused to lie to God or man even though lies were constantly told on me. I was learning how to trust God through an unfair judicial system even though I had committed the act. I knew in my heart I committed the crime to scare, not to harm, kill, or even injure individuals. The boyfriend's injury was from the bullet ricocheting off the concrete driveway was a result I had not intended. Thank God the bullet went down bounced up and only scratched the ankle making the wound superficial. Today, it is hard to envision the possibility I could have taken someone's life because of my jealousy, attitude, and temperament.

When the trial was over, I received a three year gun specification, a sentence for which I had to serve every single day. I then received a 5-15 years felonious assault charge. The verdict rendered me speechless, puzzled, and overwhelmed. Given that I had never been incarcerated before, my sentence appeared anything but fair. I was offered a plea bargain deal prior to the trial of six years flat, which I strongly rejected. I offered one year flat; in return they offered four years flat. This offer I rejected as well because it seemed too long. So I went to trial and I wound up getting more time than I would have gotten if I pled out. I was sitting in court wishing I could consider those two offers again.

Prison: In Bondage and Ensnared

After the judge sentenced me, three deputies walked towards me. I was immediately expedited to county jail and placed on murder range, due to overcrowding I presumed. Now it became real, two of my main street associates occupied the cell next to me. They were not hardcore criminals or killers as far as I knew. While a concrete wall separated us we talked. Hearing their voices made the first night there feel more familiar and a little easier. It also boosted my desire to change. Even their familiar voices did not make up for the dungeon atmosphere interwoven with the raunchy smell in the air.

Six days later, April 4, 1994, I was bussed to a holding prison where I was processed, psychologically evaluated, and stripped of material possessions, shaved hair, and indoctrinated in prison culture. This was a humiliating experience; all freedom and control was surrendered at the door. My first memorable encounter happened right as I was getting off the bus. As a Caucasian man around 5' 6" tall who was standing in line directly in front of me, got off the bus I noticed inmates gawking our way. Inmates working in the processing room started shooting sharp barbs toward this guy; about five of them began echoing loudly, "You love kids", "Your a child molester" and "Hey, you pedophile bastard." I was stunned by the way this guy was verbally attacked straight off the bus.

I was later informed that he would be my cellmate. This made me a little apprehensive, but I was humbled as I considered what Jesus would do under a similar circumstance. After going through the whole day, I found myself becoming non-judgmental of my "bunky (cell-mate)." I also, concluded ostracized inmates where pedophiles and stool pigeons (informants). He had been targeted and lambasted profusely. From this experience, I learned to allow God to judge, and that God's word does teach us to **shun profane and vain babbling: for they will increase unto more ungodliness. And their word will eat as doth a canker" 2 Ti. 2:16, 17a KJV).** That night, I lay on my top bunk in darkness meditating then praying fervently for myself and others. This would be the second time I asked the Lord to reveal Himself to me to show me if he was real. I told Him if He would, I would never doubt Him again. God first revealed Himself to me while living in my brother's fiancée's apartment when I was facing spirits of divination with drugs as a result of drug use. During this revelation, I was operating under the spirits of anger, spite, cruelty, hate, revenge, accusations, strife and rage. It was ugly. God revealed Himself the exact way with an intense piercing bright light comparable to a star. This was an awe-inspiring supernatural moment. It was God, and it is real to me. From this day forward, I have not doubted or questioned God's faithfulness.

During the encounter, God also brought to my remembrance some words my mother- in-law told me in early 1990,"One day you're going to have to eat some humble pie." At the time, I didn't think what she said was warranted and considered her words a slap in the face. First of all, I did not even know what humble pie was. In fact, I thought she had me confused with somebody else. Humble pie didn't even sound good to me, not to mention I didn't think anyone could make me eat it. But during this God-encounter, the word of James 4:10 (KJV) came to me, **"Humble yourselves in the sight of the Lord, and He shall lift you up."**

The light bulb came on as to what is meant by "eating humble pie," you see, God had already humbled me, now it was time for me to eat a slice of that pie daily. I realized that God was preparing me for this prison journey. I remained humble even when other inmates took my humbleness for weakness. I realized in my heart I had to trust God as I went through this system. I discovered that night that God is faithful even when I am not. In fact, God is faithful when I am faithless. In a matter of days, my "bunky" was taken out to another institution for security control reasons. I remained grateful for what God had shown me during my brief encounter with a man whom others had so ostracized.

As time went on, I became more observant than ever of my surrounding, fellow inmates, and the prison staff. The big square matching buildings were white on the outside full of steel bars, bricks, and stainless steel inside. We were herded to breakfast, lunch, and dinner daily. We were only given ten minutes to eat, which was uncomfortable. The first night, I was able to sleep well because God comforted me. The meals were tolerable only because there was nothing else to eat. For the most part, the corrections officers' mentality was "once a prisoner always a prisoner". The majority of them appeared to esteem themselves more highly than ought. These officers apparently did not know that scripture which says**"Not to think of yourselves more highly than he ought to think."(Romans 12:3 KJV).** It was standard protocol for us to be counted every hour on the hour, and sometimes more frequently. During the counts, we had to stand in front of our bunks or cell doors for minutes on end until told otherwise.

The cells received only dim light from a small wall plated glass, and were furnished with a small stainless steel open toilet and sink. Each 8 by

6 feet cell had a bunk bed attached to the concrete wall. The noise level was constant, piercing with vulgar language round the clock. New inmates went nowhere alone; they were escorted by prison guards. While each inmate was responsible and accountable for their own area and behavior, one bad apple could ruin the whole bushel. There was a prison inside of the prison for the non-submissive called segregation or the hole. Very little time was allowed for recreation or library use. We could not receive visitors because you never knew when you would be transported to your assigned penitentiary.

Because of overcrowding, I could look out or down my cell and see a makeshift dorm right on the main floor. Fights, arguments, and foolishness took place daily. I realized that prison was just like I heard about out on the streets. Inmates would pull up on you with con, manipulation, game, and even intimidation tactics to strike fear among other reasons. I was familiar with the personalities I had encountered because I came from the streets and had the same wilderness mentality. I am glad I went to prison with Jesus, the ugliness I saw would have fed into my former self. Prison was a good place for me to be taught humility, forgiveness, and self-denial. I had built solid walls of bitterness, resentment, and jealousy which had to be torn down. When I got to prison, I questioned God for placing me there, but asked Him, "God you guide me through my new reality." I was not comfortable being around a bunch of men who had similar wilderness mindsets that I was trying to release. God spoke to me through his Word, ***"For I know the thoughts that I think toward you, saith the Lord, thoughts of peace, and not of evil, to give you an expected end" (Jeremiah 29:11 KJV).***

Though I did not understand these words, it sounded comforting and I accepted it.

At forty-five years old, incarcerated and separated from family and supposedly friends, I began a new experience. Prisons were not a nice place nor were the people there, but I trusted God and believed that He would see me through. Besides reception, prison was only temporary. I had heard there was more freedom in the assigned prison. That was comforting news to me while I was stuck in this restrictive, overcrowded burrow of sin.

Approximately thirty days after my arrival, I was informed I'd be taken to the prison which would be my "home" for the remainder of my sentence. Even though I didn't know where I would be taken (this was kept confidential for security reasons)I was still enthusiastic about the news and was able to maintain a positive mindset. I was not thinking about escaping or adding to my imprisoned circumstances. Honestly, I was praying my new spot would give me more freedom like I had heard. The next morning, I was handcuffed to other inmates who were being transported to various penitentiaries throughout lower Southern Ohio. Though I have no recollection of the route taken, having the window seat allowed me to enjoy the beauty of God's creation. We stopped at two penitentiaries for drop offs before my stop which was the London Correctional Institution. I could see that this was an old prison. It was enormous in acreage and structurally all brick and steel with massive barbwire which enclosed the building and much of the land around its perimeter. After entering the prison, shackled hands and feet at first appearance, I had a flashback. The setting was surreal; the halls were tall, lengthy, the long hallways shiny. There were few rooms offsetting, and when looking up the hall, there was a view of the metal stairwells. The stairwells led into dorms. The entire building was eerie, cold, and dim. There was concrete and metal all around. I was reminded of old Edward G. Robinson and James Cagney prison movies such as *Black Tuesday*, *Larceny Inc.*, *The Last Gangster*, *Two Seconds* and *Kiss Tomorrow Goodbye*. This place was built in 1913 and it looked like it. It housed 1,600 inmates during my incarceration. Because it was originally a prison farm, many inmates did farm work at minimal wages receiving seventeen to twenty four dollars a month for maintaining the facility. It was a close security prison and one of Department of Rehabilitation & Correction's least costly to operate. There were isolation cells for inmates who broke rules for punishment. This first night I slept in a dorm with around 175 other inmates. We slept in bunks in a row. The six rows ran twenty beds each vertically and ten rows ran six beds horizontally each. Despite being around all those other inmates amazingly I had sweet sleep, I was assured by God's word, **"When thou liest down, thou shalt not be afraid: yea, thou shalt lie down, and thy sleep shall be sweet." (Proverbs 3:24 KJV).** I was so thankful I had the presence of God with and in me and remembered the words of scripture which say that **"because greater is He who is in you, than he that is in the world!" (1John 4:4b).**

The prison offered only a few educational programs: barbering, meat cutting and Culinary Arts. There was also an array of anger management, parenting, Alcoholics Anonymous, and other self-help courses. Thankfully, there were also several diverse church meetings offered. London had an enormous indoor gym which featured a boxing program the first year I was there. The prison had a gigantic commissary where inmates could purchase various items once a week. In the outside yard was a large concrete weight area with weights, pull-up bars, and workout areas. But after word got out that the inmates were getting too strong, the weights were declared weapons of mass destruction and banned in 1995. Connected to the yard was an enormous baseball field with a jogging track around the perimeter. Barbwire expanded beyond as far as the human eye could see. On the opposite side of the huge building was a smaller yard where inmates could walk, talk, read, and hold one on one discussions. We could only congregate in pairs and could not go into other buildings and dorms. In addition, the institution had a pretty big library filled mostly with legal textbooks, a huge cattle farm, vegetable garden, as well as a cemetery in the distance.

The prison was three and a half hours from my home and I was aware of the strain that the travel time and the cost of phone calls would place on others. So, I didn't have visitors or outside communication. Yet and still, I felt a greater sense of freedom there. I took ownership of my situation this was my affliction to bear.

Having a bunk by the window allowed me to start every morning and evening watching God orchestrate the most amazing sunrises and sunsets I ever imagined. Just fixating on the firmaments of his creation empowered my faith. I began developing my spiritual formation within community. I began working on spiritual disciplines inwardly, outwardly, and with other believers. Inwardly, **"study to show thyself approved unto God, a workman that needeth not to be ashamed, rightly dividing the word of truth." (2 Timothy 2:15 KJV).** I was now learning and sharpening my meditation skills. My prayer life was in its developmental stages, and I had picked up a commentary on the seven ways to pray to assist. Also, I began to fast, something I'd not done before. I had much work to do and being in prison gave me the time to do it.

Outwardly, I needed simplicity in my life. The word says, *"The entrance of thy words giveth light; it giveth understanding unto the simple."* *(Psalm 119:130 KJV).* All my life, I was a simple person who complicated things with my own understanding. I never had order in my life; things were pretty much chaotic. I believe my former lifestyle and worldly way of thinking contributed to my imbalanced body, soul, and mind. Through scripture, I gained a better understanding of what it means to *"lean not unto thine own understanding; in all thy ways acknowledge him, and he shall direct thy paths."* *(Proverbs 3:5, 6 KJV).*

Within a couple of weeks, I noticed that I had begun to develop a peaceful solitude within my sin sick soul. I had learned the discipline of submission in the prison work world, but practicing it with prison staff was the ultimate challenge. Being of service for the kingdom of God was a new beginning for me. I wanted to know my calling, job, and election within God's economy. Finally, on the corporate level of discipline, I found that confessing my faults to others was key. *"Confess your faults one to another, and pray one for another,"* *(James 5:16 KJV).* I was familiar with scripture which says, *"If we confess our sins, (TO GOD), he is faithful and just to forgive us our sins, and to cleanse us from all unrighteousness,"* *(1John 1:9 KJV.)* But, I didn't know who I should share my shortcomings with. I had interpreted the scripture to mean that I needed to confess to my Christian friends. But after further study, I learned that God Himself was the only true friend and I needed to confess my sins to Him.

My routine included going to church weekly, being a hearer and doer of God's Word, and examining myself daily. To maintain balance internally and externally, I jogged, walked, and dabbled with light weights and nautilus equipment. *"For bodily exercise profiteth little: but godliness is profitable unto all things, having promise of the life that now is, and of that which is to come" (1 Timothy 4:8 KJV).* By 1995, I began writing thoughts, emotions, and spiritual experiences in my memoir. My relationship with God had become established; He was the only true friend I could trust. I felt secure that he would never leave nor forsake me and would give me the unfailing love I desperately desired.

I watched very little T.V., made one phone call to my spiritual advisor, and received no visits my first two years. I also did physical chores cleaning three small in-dorm offices for $17.00 monthly. I had the position for two years, and used it as an opportunity to earn trust and show integrity.

At the end of the two years, my spiritual life had grown at a rapid pace. I was a living example that *"The Lord is nigh unto them that are of a broken heart; and saveth such as be of a contrite spirit." (Psalms 34:18 KJV).* I was catapulted to a new level of spiritual maturity by understanding Romans 12:2 KJV *"And be not conformed to this world: but be ye transformed by the renewing of your mind, that ye may prove what is that good, and acceptable, and perfect, will of God."*

I was able to measure my spiritual growth by the way I thought. My old way of thinking began to seem like pure nonsense. I am a witness that *"There is a way which seemeth right unto a man, but the end thereof are the ways of death. leads" (Proverbs 14:12 and 16:25 KJV).* Before I was in Christ, I was spiritually dead. The more I read, studied, and prayed, the more God would discharge knowledge from his Word and reveal more of Himself to me. I began to understand the meaning of agape, or unconditional love, which was bringing me into spiritual ripeness and a more in-depth understanding of His purpose for my life. During this time, God revealed His purpose for my life which was to nurture my relationship with Him in order to equip me to serve other's was God's purpose for my life. It was becoming real *"howbeit that was not first which is spiritual, but that which is natural; and afterward that which is spiritual." (1 Corinthians 15:46 KJV).* I was now allowing God who is spirit through faith and His word to develop my spiritual man. *"But God hath revealed them unto us by his spirit: for the Spirit searcheth all things"; "Now we have received, not the spirit of the world, but the spirit which is of God" (1 Corinthians 2:10, 12a KJV).* I was becoming a natural man who had been spiritually reborn, and I was completely okay with it. I had made a vow to the Lord to serve Him if He brought me out of the mess I perpetrated. Soon after, I was led to the scripture *"When thou vowest a vow unto God, defer not to pay it; fir He hath no pleasure in fools: pay that which thou hast vowed. Better is it that thou shouldest not vow, than that shouldest vow and not pay. (Ecclesiastes 5:4, 5 KJV).* My commitment was solidified and there was no way to undo what I had vowed.

Overall, the experience was challenging and uncomfortable. I am clear however that my life in prison was pivotal in my spiritual transformation from my transgressions into my righteous future. I have three memorable events that I will share from my two years at London Prison.

The first incident occurred in 1994, the year I arrived at London. I witnessed a young man being approached on the far side of the yard. As he was attempting to enter his dorm building, this guy perching in the corner cut him off at the door. I was working out and could hear the aggressor ask the victim something like, "It's been two weeks. Where is my money and my packs (cigarettes)? The victim responded that he hadn't gotten any money on the books yet. The aggressor immediately began punching, stabbing, and then kicking the victim unmercifully after which he ran off into the building. By the time the correctional officers arrived, the victim was a bloody mess. Immediately, sirens went off meaning that the yard closed and all inmates had to go back to their dorms to be in lock down. These types of violent acts happened frequently during my time.

A second incident that sticks out in my mind occurred in 1995, and involved a young man who was housed in my dorm. I had befriended him; we played basketball together. He evidently got caught up with some of his homies and got access to a bad batch of hooch (homemade alcohol) which caused him to have a fatal heart attack. We guys who lived in the dorm were saddened because he did not have long before his release. My sadness was heightened because I knew he'd been buried in the prison cemetery with no one in attendance. While sad, events such as these helped me to stay focused on Jesus and the plan God had for my life. I was learning not only about who I was, but whose HE was. I began to identify with the scripture,*"Therefore if any man be in Christ, he is a new creature: old things are passed away; behold, all things are become new."* *(2Corinthians 5:17 KJV).* My seared conscious was now being redeveloped. I was able to show empathy and concern for others. I was not bitter about where I was, but instead saw it as an opportunity for growth, ministry and learning. I showed an increased wisdom in the behaviors, decisions and choices I made. The third episode involved me and our afternoon shift Corrections Officer (CO). When I first arrived, I had put in for transfers at two other institutions because I assumed I would not be content around so many young boys, gangs, old fools, and nonsense everyday. To qualify for a status drop which was close security to minimum, I had to meet certain criteria: amount of time served, the type of criminal offense, and prison behavioral record. I worked really hard to meet all the criteria for a transfer.

But one particular day, our Correction Officer for some reason decided to attack me verbally. God had shown me favor with his superiors and he was aware of that. I had had no problems with this officer or any other officer in my two years stint at London. I was aware of this officer's shady demeanor and the favoritism he showed to his "Leroy's" or boys. Well, he ordered me to my bunk for a locker box search. I was okay with that because I did not partake in contraband or illegal paraphernalia because those were kinds of activities that would delay one's release or could hinder a status drop. Contraband ranged from a book to a pencil, depending on how the officer chose. I was discerning that this "CO"was seeking to wake up the natural man with the spirit of fear and intimidation. He was trying my fleshly man to come out. The officer began grand standing, tearing my bed apart and throwing my personal belongings out of my locker box. I was pretty heated but did not say anything, but I am sure my non-verbal communication was telling the story. He took my bibles and tossed them on the floor and continued to try to get a rise out of me. He then kicked my bed out of position and turned and walked away. The dorm was full and all eyes were on me like a giant television screen. I suddenly walked up one aisle towards his desk seething within and ready to lose it but God… I began quoting various scriptures under my breath *"no weapon formed against me shall prosper," "For God hath not given me the spirit of fear"* and *"Thou shalt not be afraid of the terror by night, nor the arrow that flieth by day."* I really wanted to punch this guy but then I thought I do not have to accept anything that is not from God. While still pacing it came to me that I was facing spiritual warfare which had nothing to do with the fleshly guard. *"For wrestle not against flesh and blood, but against principalities, against powers, against the rulers of darkness of this world, against spiritual wickedness in high places" (Ephesians 6:12 KJV).* So I walked back to my bunk, made my bed, and put everything back in place. I then walked back out of the dorm to the small yard where I prayed until dinner. This was yet another lesson in my learning how to eat "humble pie" in front of others. God confirmed for me the following day by speaking to me just like he had Daniel: *"Then said he unto me, fear not, Daniel: for from the first day that thou didst set thine heart to understand, and to chasten thyself before thy God, thy words were heard, and I am come for thy words.; (Daniel 10:12 KVJ).*

The following morning, an office clerk told me to report to the Captain's office in my dorm directly after breakfast. I assumed it was regarding the incident from the previous day. When I entered the Captain's office, he handed me some papers showing that I was a good worker who required little supervision. I was courteous, pleasant, and worked without complaint or hesitation. Then he asked if I still wanted to be transferred to a prison closer to my home city. He then informed me that my status dropped to minimum level 1 which qualified me for a minimum security institution. I was granted the right to be transferred to Trumbull Correctional Institution (TCI), thirty minutes from home, Youngstown, Ohio. This prison had recently built an honor camp in the back of the facility, which I was qualified to live-in because I was a model prisoner. My response was a resounding yes. I thanked the Captain. More than that, I thanked him for his favor. I rejoiced in my heart saying, *"O taste and see that the Lord is good: blessed is the man that trusteth in Him" (Psalm 34:8 KJV).* I signed some papers, and it was a done deal. Two days later, after twenty-two months, I was transferred from London Prison and up north to my new "holding pattern." This situation confirmed for the scripture that *"all things work together for the good to them that love God, to them who are the called according to his purpose" (Romans 8:28 KJV).* I am a living witness that good things will come out of negative situations. I live by this adage.

I left London comforted in times of regret and guided in times of tribulation. Through God's grace, I grew in humility which was very different from how I was used to handling confrontation. I thank God for the gift of meekness, strength under control I began learning to view fleshly clashes as spiritual battles and attaining spiritual victories. Also, I had also gained the ability to comprehend that it is through the power of

God's words that victory is won. I began to embody the scripture which says, *"Ye received it not as the word of men, but as it is in truth, the word of God which effectually worketh also in you that believe (1 Thessalonians 2:13 KJV).* The Lord was unveiling His unconditional and unfailing love, the love I have always desired in a myriad of ways. **His love was different** from the so called love I had known, which cusses, bickers, and fights. *"Charity suffereth long, and is kind; charity envieth not; charity vaunteth not itself, is not puffed up, doth not behave itself unseemly, seeketh not her own, is not easily provoked, thinketh no evil; rejoiceth not in iniquity, but rejoiceth in the truth; beareth all things, believeth all things, hopeth all things, endureth all things (1 Corinthians 13:4-8 KJV).* The Lord had torn down some walls of bitterness, aggression, jealousy, and hatred. He had brought me a mighty long way in a short period of time. Despite my growth, I knew I had a mighty long way to go in becoming genuinely, totally, and completely free,*"If the Son therefore shall make you free, ye shall be free indeed." (John 8:36 KJV).* I would never forget that two short years prior, I came to Christ with no strength. *Therefore I take pleasure in infirmities, in reproaches, in necessities, in persecutions, in distress for Christ' sake: for when I was weak, then am I strong."(2 Corinthians 12:10 KJV).* I was developing moral strength in Christ along this tedious journey. I realized *"For without me ye can do nothing"(John 15:3b KJV)*but fail, wobble in hurt, and hurt others. To God be the Glory!

Leaving London was just another step in my spiritual process. I still needed much more pruning.

"Every branch in me that beareth not fruit he taketh away: and every branch that beareth fruit, he purgeth it, that it may bring forth more fruit."

(John 15:2 KJV) Having retired from the Illuminating Company in Forestry, I was fully aware of the pruning process. Pruning could mean life or death to a tree or bush, and pruning phases could look ugly or detrimental in unskilled hands. So whether I topped it, rounded over, side trimmed, under trimmed, center trimmed or just shaped to the situation; my goal was not only for it to look good but to ultimately, allow the power lines to bring forth energy and light. I had come to learn, witness, and testify that pruning is painful to the "tree," human or otherwise, being pruned. But as I pruned, I saw the, renewal, replenishing, and revitalizing those trees just as I was seeing with my own life in Christ.

> *"And ye shall know the truth, and the truth shall*
> *make you free." (John 8:32 KJV).*

Part of the pruning process for me was to admit the truth of my sins. The realization that my life was unmanageable and I was on my way to hell was disturbingly painful. I thanked the Lord that as I surrendered daily and allowed God to expose and begin pruning my sins away. The pain of some of my sin was horrific, but eventually subsided. I still have some scars but the pain, if any, is not anyway as severe after the healing process is completed*"And with his stripes we are healed" (Isaiah 53:5c KJV).*

After arriving at Trumbull Correctional Institution (TCI) on January 26, 1996, the processing was pretty much the same as before but was simpler, smoother and less congested. The facility was not nearly as large nor was there a big prison adjacent to the prison camp. . The institution was one story, with no stairs anywhere. There were only two neighboring dorms A and B which held 220 inmates at full capacity each. Each dorm had significant shower stalls partitioned, toilets, and sinks with metal mirrors. It was also extremely clean, and the heating was good. There were no rats, roaches, or pigeons living "rent free."

There was more freedom. With permission only inmates could visit the opposite dorm. Permission was normally permitted. There were various rooms for visiting, meeting, church room, library, small weight room, and dining hall all within the one building. There were also two professional-size pool tables in each dorm. The yard was much smaller than the one at London; it had a baseball field and two full-size basketball courts. . There was also a small jogging track. . Things were definitely better here, and a lot quieter. *"Unto the upright there ariseth light in the darkness: he is gracious, and full of compassion, and righteous. (Psalm 112:4 KJV).* Even so, I was still in prison (the sin den). I had no clue when this voyage would be over because I had not finished serving the three-year conviction. I was denied my appeal for less time. However, even before actually being in contact with my children, being here made me feel close to my family especially my sons and daughter.

Although the location was different, negative mindsets were not. The spiritual warfare was tantamount, if not worse. The battleground and spiritual warfare heightened in this new place. To me, it appeared the inmates doing life sentences ran the camp and increased tensions. Just being in proximity with men who would never get out of prison, challenged my resolve. I was self-determined to stay on the Christian walk. There were men with wilderness mentalities all around me. They had already done 15 to 20 years, and their outlook appeared gloomy.

While at TCI, the Lord continued bestowing favor on me. *"For whoso findeth me findeth life, and shall obtain favour of the Lord." (Proverbs 8:35 KJV).* I was granted a wall bed in the back row, free from all traffic. Unlike London Prison, each row was partitioned by a four feet divider wall allowing better privacy. There were far less lock downs, fights, and infringements. The inmates could get to know each other better, flaws and all. Some inmates were seeking change in their lives; others were fine with life the way it was. I knew far more inmates personally, had a larger fellowship of Christian brothers, and engaged in sustained bible study.

I worked a number of jobs during my time. At first, I was given the job of cleaning the small nurses' office directly outside my dorm. It was a good job with no weekends and flexible hours. After a year, I was promoted to the main prison business office. I worked for $24.00 a month as the only copy clerk and business office porter. I was free to walk through the gates unassisted daily. In 1999, I began working as a motivational speaker for projects at high schools and detention centers. My last six months, I was given a "road crew worker position. We traveled the entire Trumbull County area picking up trash on the highways and at the Trumbull County Fair. Far as me being able to work with such freedom was not a mystery; I understood what God was doing. He was preparing me for release. This was a promise of God:*"Let not mercy and truth forsake thee: bind them about thy neck; write them upon the table of thine heart: so shalt thou find favor and good understanding in the sight of God and man." (Proverbs 3:3-4 KJV).* The more rigorously I focused on serving God, the more He gave me favor with others when I needed it most. My plan remained the same after becoming saved and trust the One who created me, His plan for me is good.

In addition to getting involved in the same things I had when I was at London, I also became enmeshed in various programs. This included becoming Chairperson of Narcotic Anonymous (NA), referee for the under 40 years old basketball league and bible study teacher. Teaching from the bible helped me to learn and understand. It allowed the power of the Holy Spirit to guide me in discerning all that pertained to life and godliness. One specific area I focused on was the fruit of the spirit. ***"But the fruit of the spirit is love, joy, peace, longsuffering, gentleness, goodness, faith, meekness, temperance" (Galatians 5:22-23 KJV).***

In 1996, my yearning to make strides in my spiritual life intensified. This happened in prison during results of a number of life events: visits, deaths, and sports. This was the year I received my first visit from my wife and three children. Seeing them was highly emotional because I had been separated from them since 1993. It was extremely painful knowing that being separated from them was the result of my poor choices. I took ownership of the disconnection because it was my fault. It hurt to know that I had left my children fatherless.

It also pained me to see that my wife had made the trip to visit me with her boyfriend. She wrote me a letter in 1995, telling me to "get a life." Her statement propelled me to change and to become a better father. Even though I had come to the realization in London that the marriage was over, I didn't like seeing my wife or our kids with another man.

While I was hurt and insensitive to others' feelings, God was working on me. I knew prayer was the central way for God to transform me and them. I believed the Lord could hear my prayers and that those prayers changed my life and continue to until this day. God is Omnipotent, the supreme power and authority; Omnipresent; Omniscience, I trusted in the Lord in all situations and things. I was totally dependent on Him. ***"And he answering said, thou shalt love the Lord thy God with all thy heart; and with all thy soul, and with all thy strength, and with all thy mind; and thy neighbor as thyself" (Luke 10: 27 KJV).*** I knew I was inwardly being changed and did not feel the need to have to prove anything. I was evolving away from being a people pleaser. God had also delivered me from cussing, lying, smoking, drugs, alcohol, and gambling. While in London Prison, I made a covenant with God just as Job had made. I was feeling good about who I was in Christ, who he was in me and what I was doing in His sight. Despite the emotional difficulty, the visit ended in love and concern for family. I proceeded back to my bunk space and began thinking about my next visit with my three older sons. I was concerned about how my bad choices had affected my relationship with them.

Soon after, I received a visit from my eldest and youngest son by my first wife. When I first saw them, I instantly had congenial feeling toward them, but I also imagined what it must have felt like having an uninvolved father like I was. The visit helped to begin to bond again. It appeared as though my older son was more empathetic to what I was going through. I had yet felt total forgiveness. I needed to better understand before praying and giving over to God.

I discovered from the visits that being separated from loved ones was painfully agonizing. No family member or outsider could fully comprehend my suffering and losses and understood its depth. My pastor would say, "God did His job, (God's will) then sent His Son as an example (to perform

His will). It is Christ's shed blood that brings spiritual life for those who believe He died and was then resurrected. He ascended to heaven. *"But the comforter, which is the holy ghost, whom the father will send in my name, He shall teach you all things, andHe shall teach you all things, and bring all things to your remembrance, whatsoever I have said unto you."* *(John 14:26 KJV).* By faith, the Holy Spirit empowers the believer and gives him a new life. Jesus said, *"And I will pray the Father, and He shall give you another comforter that he may abide with you for ever; even the spirit of truth. (John 14:16, 17a KJV).* The Holy Spirit helps us in all affinities, afflictions, loss and all things. I learned loss could ultimately make one better or bitter, I chose to be better. I was now allowing the Holy Spirit to do His job, change me.

In 1995, it also marked the year I experienced the pain of death. In early March of that year, on a phone conversation with my oldest son, he disclosed that my aunt who lived across from me had passed away. My auntie, who is of Philippine heritage, was unique and special in my life and the lives of the rest of our family members. Her life, traditions, and customs truly blessed me, especially the food she prepared. For the first time in my life after experiencing loss, I was aware through the Holy Spirit that it is okay to mourn. *"Blessed are they that mourn, for they shall be comforted." (Matthew 5:4 KJV).* My aunt's death validated for me that I can't control everything. Her death as well as the death of my friend in London Prison taught me to accept the highs and lows in life and seek God as a comforter. *"Have not I commanded thee? Be strong and of a good courage. Be not afraid; neither be thou dismayed: for the Lord thy God is*

with thee whithersoever thou goest, *(Joshua 1:9 KJV)* and those losses confirmed my dying daily.

I had to put on the whole armor of God the first day I stepped foot into prison. Putting it on became a daily ritual. During the summer, I played basketball daily which I loved and which allowed me to maintain my competitive spirit and physical conditioning. The difference between playing in the outside world and playing in prison was that players got angry on a regular basis. As I observed this anger, I believed it was really the only way for the inmates to vent in general. For me, basketball helped relieve tension and kept me physically fit. I also used the time to minister on the court. You see, unlike me, the majority of men used basketball as an opportunity to gamble. This usually led to cussing, quarreling, and fighting. I often told my competitors that I enjoyed beating them for free. I never lost any friendships or money over basketball.

Wearing the whole armor of God definitely came in handy. It taught me how to confront, be disciplined, and minister to others while in the field amongst tares and wheat (Matthew 13: 24-30 KJV). It also taught me three important things:*"Recompense to no man evil for evil. Provide things honest in the sight of all men." (Romans 12:17 KJV). "Finally, be ye all of one mind, having compassion one of another, love as brethren, be pitiful, be courteous; not rendering evil for evil, or railing for railing; but contrariwise blessings; knowing that ye are there unto called, that ye should inherit a blessing." (1 Peter 3:8, 9 KJV). And "as free, and not using your liberty for a cloak of maliciousness, but as the servants of God. Honor all men. Love the brotherhood. Fear God. Honour the King".(1Peter 2: 16, 17 KJV).* The basketball court turned out to be a good place to glorify God through my life's example.

For the first time in my life, I had an indescribable feeling of personal accomplishment in basketball. A few weeks before signing up for the 40 and over basketball league, I became the number one draft pick throughout the camp. I was also near the top of the seven other coaches' draft lists. Making the game winning points to put us in the playoffs was another highlight of my basketball career. I began playing there at forty-six, and God blessed me to be able to play until age fifty-seven. Basketball enhanced me physically and increased my awareness of my body as the temple of the Holy Ghost. ***"Beloved, I wish above all things that thou mayest prosper and be in health, even as thy soul prospereth." (3 John 1:2 KJV)***

When the season was over, many inmates recommended me for one of the few referee positions. It did not occur to me that the forty and under league would be more violent. I accepted the challenge with the aspiration of being honest and fair to the best of my God-given ability. It never occurred to me that not everyone viewed basketball as a game, but rather as a hustle. The gambling element was particularly strong among lifers, as was the level of anger.

I learned that anger was natural and men would perceive love with elements of confusion or misconception. Our love was very seldom congruent with our behavior. A man's love is at times affiliated with some degree of motive, loss, work, and sexually motivated. Our love in many instances is distorted by view of self, lack of self-esteem, and dependency on the woman or others. In many instances, our environment, world view, culture, and relationships wreak havoc on our ability to love. In the final analysis, if a person does not love God who is love, it is hard to imagine one truly loving anyone.*"Beloved, let us love one another, for love is God; and everyone that loveth is born of God, and knoweth God. He that loveth not knoweth not God; for God is Love." (1 John 4:7,8 KJV).*

There were constant altercations at the basketball games. As a referee, I was required to use a multitude of skills such as peace-making, intervention, and rule regulator. Refereeing prison basketball was very risky as well as challenging to one's well-being.

During my third game of the season, one lifer who didn't like my call began loudly shouting obscenities in an attempt to intimidate me. I walked purposely up court to get away from him and keep the peace. When I turned back around, this inmate was walking aggressively towards me continuing his cussing. Through my peripheral vision, I noticed the whole yard of inmates standing still. There were some even gazing out from the only two doorways. I knew I had to stand my ground. It was absolutely quiet in the yard, except for his loud cursing. Before I knew it, he was up close in my face spewing out his verbal crap. I just stood there attempting to explain how I saw the play. I could see this guy was enraged and was trying to provoke me into reacting. I had used my only newly God-given defusing skill, walking away. Then he spat in my face. At that point, I was ready to explode with anger I had flashbacks.

One of the first lessons I'd learned on the street is that nobody spits on you. But God's grace humbled, and though I felt like responding in the flesh, I didn't. That was nothing but God. I walked away with the entire yard astonished. It was only Jesus that I didn't react like I would have in the streets. Instead, I maintained a different character than I had on the street. After the incident, many men commended me on how I'd handled the situation. I shared with them it wasn't me, but God that deserved the glory. *"I am the Lord: that is my name: and my glory will I not give to another, neither my praise to graven images (Isaiah 42:8 KJV)* and *"I am crucified with Christ: nevertheless live; yet not I, but Christ liveth in me: and the life which I now live in the flesh I live by the faith of the son of God, who loved me, and gave himself for me." (Galatians 2:20 KJV).*

Later that evening, I went to the B-dorm to confront this guy in love. I did not stay long, but I had **harbored no wrongs (1Corinthians 13:5 KJV)** and forgave him. I apologized and he did too. I was able to minister to him. Soon after, God removed him all together. Through this incident, I was learning to give respect even when I thought others didn't deserve it, merely because God commands it. I was reminded of the story of Joseph how his brothers hated him, thought to kill him but sold him. They then stripped him, abandoned him, and left him waterless to die. When I think of how wrong they treated their own biological brother, but that he forgave them. Joseph definitely chose to be **better not bitter.** The incident at the basketball game was yet another simple teachable moment on God's love, forgiveness, mercy, and respect of others as God's creation. *"But as for you, ye thought evil against me; but God meant it unto good, to bring to pass, as it is this day, to save much people alive" (Genesis. 50:20 KJV).*

Four months into 1997, the 3-year gun specification sentence behind me, I had a paradigm shift. I reflected on God's goodness and where he had brought me from, where I was, and how far I had to go. I had an epiphany.

I was not doing all this time for this particular crime; rather I was reaping consequences for the years of past sins. I was reaping what I had sown and paying a stern cost for my mess. *"Be not be deceived; God is not mocked: For whatsoever a man soweth, that shall heal so reap. For he that soweth to his flesh shall of the flesh reap corruption; but he that soweth to the spirit shall of the spirit reap life everlasting." (Galatians 6:7,8 KJV).* It was okay with me because I wanted all past mistakes behind and my sowing spiritual things were now paying dividends to God, His kingdom, and myself. I began thinking how God was making relevant all my discouragement and discomfort throughout my life. It was my experiential God showing me how," *If a man therefore purge himself from these, he shall be a vessel unto honour, sanctified, and meet for the master's use, and prepared unto every good work."(2 Timothy 2:21 KJV).* He was preparing me for the ministry of encouraging and comforting others. I had experienced significantly dissuasion and uneasiness. I had experienced a lot as a result of much sin, specifically longsuffering, broken heartiness, resentment, and more. I was truly enjoying life today even though I was in prison. I was being untangled day by day.

I could relate to how the Apostle Paul must have felt during this time in prison. *"He hath sent me to bind up the broken hearted, to proclaim liberty to the captives and the opening of the prison to them that are bound." (Isaiah 61:1b KJV).* Though I was locked up physically, I was free in my mind and my soul was resting; there were no more dark clouds over me. I thank God for freeing me, Hallelujah!!! *"And calleth those things which be not as though they were." (Romans 4:17 KJV).* I was still claiming my release from physical prison, but I was still free on the inside I had enough faith to understand if I continued trusting in the Lord and continued to be obedient I would be free mind, body, and soul. The new thought of genuinely, totally, and completely being free was extremely stimulating. My philosophy which I shared with other inmates was, "It is better to have Jesus in prison than not to have Jesus out there in the world." I conveyed to others that it is better to know Jesus and not need Him than to need Him and not know Him. Having my flesh hold my mind captive to sin was not new to me, but holding my thoughts captive to the obedience to Christ was *"Casting down imaginations, and every high thing that exaltheth itself against the knowledge of God, and bringing into captivity every thought to the obedience of Christ." (2 Corinthians 10:5 KJV).*

Prison had become a school of higher learning for me. I wanted to graduate with honors. I did not want to repeat any lessons, or journey down a path that would ever cause me to revert back to prison or sin. I thank God I came to prison with a teachable and humble spirit, doing everything in reverence to the Lord. *"And whatsoever ye do, do it heartily, as to the Lord, and not unto men;" (Colossians 3:23 KJV).*

Now having some God sense, I continued to allow walls to be torn down in my life. While I spent 1997, I began a phrase of advanced spiritual development, which I discerned was in preparation for ministry. I did not know what ministry, even though I was already teaching, witnessing, and ministering. I realized that I needed to continue to cultivate these gifts so that I would be ready. *"Sow to yourselves in righteousness, reap in mercy; break up your fallow ground; for it is time to seek the Lord, till he come and rain righteousness upon you." (Hosea 10:12 KJV).* I always wondered why God placed me around irrational, irritable, and obnoxious people. God showed me through His word, ***"For God is not unrighteous to forget your work and labour of love, which ye have shown toward His name, in that ye have ministered to the saints, and do minister."(Hebrews 6:10 KJV)***. I began to understand the experiences of prison, school, and on the job training, as training for ministry. The work God was preparing me for was not for the timid or faint of heart. ***"Wherefore I put thee in remembrance that thou stir up the gift of God, which is in thee by the putting on of my hands. For God hath not given us the spirit of fear; but of power, and of love, and of a sound mind." (2 Timothy 1:6-7 KJV).***

My transformation continued into 1997. I was learning and understanding that my changing required me to deny myself, die to my flesh and humble myself. This change also required fervent and steadfast prayer and fasting in secret, as the bible teaches and experiencing pain and healing while growing in God's grace. In prison, secret places were hard to come by, so I got imaginative and walked the track perimeter, used the shower, or my bunk area as my prayer closets. These practices allowed me to see my old self in others except***"When I become a man, I put away childish things" (1 Corinthians 13:11 KJV))***.

Prison was my equivalent to Harvard University. I finally realized the state, white man, judge, nor the world owed me anything. After four years of being incarcerated, I realized that the law is for law breakers. ***"Knowing this, that the law is not made for a righteous man, but for the lawless and disobedient, for the ungodly and for sinners, for unholy and profane, for murderers of mothers, for manslayers." (1 Timothy 1:9 KJV).*** I had not just broken man-made law, but also the Law of God. This *"Prison School of Hard Knocks"* was a heart check which was beneficial for me. It was allowing me to unpack deep dark and secret things within my soul. I was becoming an attentive hearer in the God's Word *"For there is nothing, hid, which shall not be manifested; neither was anything kept secret, but that it should come abroad." (Mark 4:22 KJV).* So, I found myself unearthing and exposing those things God has redeemed me from, without guilt or shame. *"For if any be a hearer of the word, and not a doer, he is like unto a man beholding his natural face in a glass" (James 1: 23 KJV).* My 1997 spiritual development semester taught me to do what's right in God's sight. I discovered that working within the system as opposed to bucking it was a better way to go. As long as I was obedient to God's spiritual law, the systems laws, protocol, and policies were easy to follow. *"For rulers are not a terror to good works, but to evil. Wilt thou then not be afraid of the power? Do that which is good, and thou shalt have praise of the same." (Romans 13:3 KJV).* This was only possible for me because *"I can do all things through Christ who strengtheneth me" (Philippians. 4:13 KJV).*

In 1998, I became a smidgen more established in who I was, to whom I belonged, and what I was becoming in Christ. The year of 1998 was a time of educational and spiritual growth. I was learning in three worlds. First, I was figuring out how I would reenter the secular world (or the world that was) which I had left five years earlier. Secondly, there was this world of prison which I currently was residing and waiting to be set free from. Finally, there was the world I was now striving toward, the new heaven. *"Four our conversation is in heaven; from whence also we look for the Saviour, the Lord Jesus Christ." (Philippians 3:20 KJV). "Nevertheless we according to his promise, look for new heavens and a new earth, wherein dwelleth righteousness. (2 Peter 3:13 KJV).*

I was puzzled by how prison did very little to transform and rehabilitate men. Prison thrived on the passiveness and idleness of idol minds which only benefited the prison industry. If inmates changed, prisons could risk putting themselves out of business. But my mind was made up; I was bound and determined to change through my personal relationship with Jesus Christ.

I began realizing how everything I did would affect others, me, and my relationship with God. My choices and decisions were pivotal to my well being and quality of life. I was in Rome (prison), but I did not have to do what the Romans (prisoners) did. The secular and prison worlds formulate their own man-made laws, rules, and policies. Although, these regulations are necessary for those who inhabit these worlds, they may be different in all nations, countries, states, counties, cities, and townships. Because they are man-made and differentiate throughout the world, the less fortunate have no input into these laws. No one asks the lowly or those who have been disregarded what they want or how can we help you to function better, not even what's good for you. But once I began interpreting things spiritually or through the mind of Christ, I became subject to a much higher law. *"Let this mind be in you, which was also in Christ Jesus" (Philippians 2:5 KJV).* I was able to internalize that, *"There is a way which seemeth right unto a man, but theend are the ways of death." (Proverbs 14: 12 and 16:25 KJV).* Just as in the secular world, prison is designed to keep individuals downtrodden. Observing inmates continue working for the devil and doing things their way, being released and returning to prison. This weighed heavily on me, my spirit grieved. In my opinion, prison and secular authorities knew who was selling drugs, sex, and prison provisions.

They allowed it because they knew these actions would contribute to their staying behind bars or coming back. Prisoners do not have the capacity to go out and bring in street drugs and contraband. Having lived in both worlds, today my world is more peaceful, comforting, and jovial. I chose to serve the Lord and it's the best decision I have ever made thus far. I have a new life. Hallelujah! The new world or New Jerusalem, the Holy City which I've been striving toward has one authority, God. He never changes, nor does he show partiality and favoritism. His love is unconditional. *"And I heard a great voice out of heaven saying, behold, the tabernacle of God is with men, and he will dwell with them, and they shall be his people, and God himself shall be with them, and be their God. And God shall wipe away all tears from their eyes; and there shall be no more death, neither sorrow, nor crying, neither shall there be any more pain: for the former things are passed away." (Revelation 21:3, 4 KJV).* Knowing this reassured me. It is profound to me to know I am going to be dead longer than I will be alive and that spiritually, I will live never to die again. Jesus said, *"The thief cometh not, but for to steal, and to kill and to destroy; I am come that they might have life, and that they might have it more abundantly." (John 10:10 KJV).* Just before the end of 1998, I experienced another defining moment. I had come back in the camp from work and headed to my bunk area. Before I could get settled, a transfer CO who I knew approached my bed and commanded me to pack up. He told me I was going to the hole, but didn't say why, except to say I was under investigation. Though stunned, I remained humble, innocent, and trusting in Jesus. I was intent on having my time in prison being drama, shock and sucker free. Having been incarcerated four years, I knew prison procedure: first, you go to the hole (isolation), then, you receive a ticket for the violation, and finally, the one being investigated sits in front of a committee. Handcuffed, I was only allowed to take my bible with me. But as God would have it on the way up top to the main prison, the officer shared that the situation related to one of my Christian brothers who had become inappropriately involved with a young woman via mail outside the prison. My name was on a paper I had helped him write. But, I was not moved *"He only is my rock and my salvation: he is my defense, I shall not be moved." (Psalm 62:6 KJV)* This may have been one of the first times in my life I did not attempt to figure out what I had done or said. It was a moment I began to put God to the test and started quoting his word *"If God be for us who can be against us" (Romans 8:31b KJV). it doesn't matter "When I cry unto thee, then shall mine enemies turn back: this I know; for God is for me." (Psalm 56:9 KJV).*

I knew this other inmate was confrontational, but I had no qualms with him. Deep in my spirit, I knew I'd had no affiliation with the brother's nonsense. While in the hole, I read constantly, meditated, and prayed as usual. Being in the hole required me to tolerate loud, continuous, and unbearable cursing and sinister noise. I maintained,*"And the peace of God which passeth all understanding, shall keep your hearts and minds through Christ Jesus" (Philippians 4:7 KJV).* After three days, I was transferred back to my dorm. I went back to my same bunk which was unheard of. But God be the glory. It was unheard of someone returning to their same bunk from segregation.

In the end, the inmate who was found guilty implicated me based on the paper I helped him write. I never encountered him again; I assume he'd been shipped out. I was never ticketed or charged, and my prison record remained untarnished.

The year of 1999 was another triumphant year for me in my spiritual journey. A number of events during this year helped me grow in God's grace and in three key Christ-like attributes. These events would be my trial by fire. First, I had a Christian lady friend who'd become my pen pal. This fellowship lasted a long time. Even though I had not met her personally and only saw vague pictures, I had developed feelings for her. I met her through a Christian "bunky" that was to be married to her sister. He shared with me she was pregnant. I felt betrayed not only by the pregnancy but because I'd learned about it from someone else. I had flashbacks of yesteryear. But quickly I remembered that she was only a friend, a fellow laborer in Christ, and a babe in Christ. I had to forgive her, but before that I had to understand mercy.*"For he shall have Judgment without mercy, that hath shown no mercy; and mercy rejoiceth against judgment."(James 2:13 KJV).* In order for me to forgive and show mercy, I had to die to self. You can only learn to forgive, if you've been in a situation where you've had to do so. Words in scriptures such as forgiveness, humility, mercy, and compassion, require action for spiritual maturity to occur. An outgrowth of spiritual maturity is the experience of peace, joy, liberty, security and comfort. God bestows these qualities on whoever believes.*"For God so loved the world that he gave his only begotten Son, that whosoever believeth in him should not perish, but have everlasting life." (John 3: 16 KJV).* Although, I only talked to her after my release a couple times, I consistently kept her and her family in prayer.

Another significant event occurred while working for the road crew community service. While on the job, I got a premonition that I would be released. Although I did not know the time or date. I did know that my parole date was less than a year away. *"For we walk by faith, not by sight" (2Corinthians 5: 7 KJV).* My confidence in God made this forewarning even more realistic. *"Now faith is the substance of things hoped for, the evidence of things not seen" (Hebrews 11:1 KJV).* I actually claimed my release instantly after I *"called those things which be not as though there were" (Romans 4: 17 KJV)* then continued my day.

When I came in camp one afternoon after work, God clearly made known to be my calling. I would be trusted with an encouraging and comforting ministry. It was all making complete sense, I was progressing in God's sense (spiritually). The longsuffering I had endured was necessary for me to get to this point in my life. You see, God had been calling me, but I always managed to ignore the call. I had always been determined to do it my way, but God chose me. Ministry is not the profession I would have chosen, but with the spiritual resources and His power I am able to stand. I reflect back on how many choices I made which led to my becoming a sinner, addict and now a criminal. I didn't want to be those things, but without God I had no power to do the right thing. On December 16, 1999, I was approached early around breakfast by my case manager, who informed me that I would be going before the furlough board that morning. That morning, I had forgotten I applied for a furlough on October 29, 1999. Although, I was not overly enthusiastic and unaware of the furlough procedures, I did know I was up for parole early next year. I remembered my premonition, claim, and supplication unto the Lord, so I eagerly changed to my interview prison garb to see what God had in store. I began thanking the Lord and determined that I was willing to take the first opportunity out of prison, regardless of any restrictions and stipulations. My lack of enthusiasm turned to thanksgiving for my imminent release.

I was fourth in line for the furlough hearing. While waiting, I carefully observed the inmates who appeared before me. By their facial expressions and body language, it appeared that they'd been rejected. Despite what I saw, I was still encouraged when my turn came. The board consisted of three people, an African American man, and a Caucasian man and women, who all appeared calm and spoke directly to me. The answers to the questions were simple; I had accepted ownership and responsibility for my actions. I had done everything asked of me and then some during my incarceration. I was humble and remorseful. My prison record was impeccable which they had before them, showed my positive attitude and work ethic.

After fifteen to twenty minutes, the committee asked if there was anything I wanted to add. I responded no, got up shook their hands and proceeded outside to await my fate. Three minutes later, I was summoned back and was told that my furlough had been denied. As I was heading back to my bunk, someone told me that I was wanted back in the boardroom. I walked back to the hearing room and knocked on the door. The board had a different look about them. Supernaturally, I witnessed, and have the documentation today to prove it, that day I saw God's hand move. I watched one of the board members cross over the denial and write and tell me I had been approved for release. I was overwhelmed. I shook everyone's hand and proceeded to the door. I felt exhilarated to an inexpressible measure. My facial countenance on the trip back to the bunk this time changed 180 degrees and I was quick to say I've been approved, Hallelujah. This was an early Christmas present. I would be released though I didn't know when. When I returned to the camp, I began sharing with my fellow inmates the attributes of Christ the Vine, which flows to the Christian, the branch. My pending release did not mean that my journey was over.

When the year 2000 came around, I was exceedingly jovial and assured of the indwelling of the Holy Spirit renewing in me daily. I encountered multiple"wannabe joy robbers" or inmates who threw stumbling blocks and obstacles in my path. But I thank God for the word of God which was *a lamp unto my feet, and a light unto my path (Psalm 119:105 KJV).* I was also grateful to God for helping me move through various temptations. Not everyone is excited for you when good things come your way. There were many who were not happy about my receiving a furlough. I came into prison by myself, knowing I would leave prison by myself. I realized the mentality of those around me was another spiritual battle. Even though the battle was not mine, I had to continue to *"work out your own salvation with fear and trembling" (Philippians 2:12 KJV).*

My work was made a bit more challenging by the death of my spiritual advisor. I had been really excited about our anticipated reunion since he was so instrumental in my early Christian walk. I wanted deeply to personally fellowship with him again. He was exceptionally knowledgeable of the Scriptures. I wanted him to see how much I had grown.

Not having an out or release date really was good because it allowed me to maintain the same humble attitude and to continue my ministry work. The Holy Spirit allowed me to continue to receive the help I could not give myself. I did not want to revert as others to clock watching and marking calendar time, that to me, is doing hard time. So I finished my time like I started my time, day by day and second by second with Jesus.

I called to inform my older sons through their mother of my good news. She told me that her dad had hired a lawyer a year ago in an attempt to bring me back to court to get me released. I was not aware of this, but it turns out the lawyer he'd hired wasn't able to complete and file the documents. But knowing this confirmed for me that God had already devised a plan for my re-entry back into society. I expressed my appreciation and gratitude for my ex-father-in-law's willingness to help me out. I was learning to *"be still and know that I am God" (Psalm 46:10 KJV).* God can use or choose anyone he wants when and however he chooses. You can learn and even be helped by any instrument or vessel God chooses, even animals. The key attribute I learned was patience and how indispensable it was in my faith walk.

On March 9, 2000, eighty-six days after my written release, I was released. Hallelujah! My patience had borne fruit. The patience I attained in prison through Christ kept me from putting myself in compromising situations and places. Knowing I could take patience with me wherever I went was inspiring. I left prison having "graduated with honors." I also left with a greater appreciation and respect for life. I also left knowing that I still had to work very hard to sustain the progress I had made once I was released. I was clearly aware that I would meet other tests, trials, and temptations when I got back into the perilous "real world." My spiritual man was prepared for applying God's word with the help of the Holy Spirit.

Despite the challenges that were before me, I was excited to reenter society. To be sure, my release was conditional. My furlough required a six month layover at a transitional facility in Cleveland, Ohio. I also had a year of parole on paper to fulfill with conditions. But, God prepared me for what was ahead. . *"But they that wait upon the Lord shall renew their strength; they shall mount up with wings as eagles" (Isaiah. 40:31 KJV).* I had been asking the Lord to teach me how to be a better man, a better father, grandfather and future husband. I realized He was not finished with me yet.

Spiritual Healing: I Can do all things which Strengthens me through Christ

On March 9, 2000, I began living in my new holding pattern where I would remain until August 1, 2000. This facility was different from prison, but there were some similar elements. For example, the residents had the same wilderness mentalities which was reflected in their drug usage (despite a zero tolerance policy) and not following other rules, such as convening in the lounge areas and dating women residents.

The facility, which was located downtown, was an old refurbished hotel which had been transformed into a transitional center. The building had twelve floors. Men in transition occupied the eighth floor which gave us a bird's eye view of downtown, crowds, and traffic. The Convocation Center at Cleveland State University sat directly across the street from the facility. Each floor catered to specific groups such as women with children, men in transition, and those in alcohol/drug recovery programs. Everyone was required to sign in and out. Everyone was subject to random alcohol/drug testing and would be evicted or sent back to prison if testing positive. We were allowed to go out in the community to work during the day, but had to be in by 8 p.m. If we broke any rules, we would be reported to the authorities since complying with the rules was mandatory. This allowed individuals to participate in this alternative program. Choosing to disobey the rules resulted in discharged or sent back to prison.

Residents on my floor had to have a work or educational plan. And though it seemed to me that the rules were simple enough to follow, a lot of residents chose not to follow them, and ended up back in prison.

My court-ordered plan was not one I would have chosen for myself, but I knew it was the plan God had for me. I was required to attend a 16-week anger management program and a monthly visit to my parole officer. For me, furlough and parole were simple. All I had to do was stay away from alcohol, drug users, come in on time, and follow the itinerary. I was also very disciplined and only followed leaders who were about God's business. While others were doing Satan's business, I was still engaged in preparation and engaged in intensive training mode. My goal was to be about my Father's business. Be about my Father's interests in light of all he had done for me. Even though I could never repay him, I felt obligated to give him my all in all. I had endured longsuffering and was okay with it, but I would not revert back to suffering for wrong. ***"Forasmuch then as Christ hath suffered for us in the flesh, arm yourselves likewise with the same mind, for he that hath suffered in the flesh hath ceased from sin" (1 Peter 4:1 KJV).***

I continued my daily routines of praying and studying God's word. In addition, I spent time walking through downtown and learned how to navigate the bus system. During my stay there, I also had the opportunity to expand my work in ministry. Under the direction of a husband and wife team, last named McKay, both Salvation Army captains, I assisted with church meetings, preaching, reading scripture, and praying. I also met Mr. and Mrs. Barrett who facilitated Wednesday bible studies, and was given the task of facilitating in their absence. During my time at this facility, I was allowed to pursue my purpose and God's plan for His kingdom. I became extremely close to the McKay's and the Barrett's, and they would be influential in my future.

After a month of acclimating back into the "real" world, I discovered that the world had changed quite a bit. Computers, cell phones and debit cards were among these that were new to me. It took a little getting used to and was somewhat overwhelming, but with a little patience, humility and an open mind, I made out okay.

In addition to the challenges of adjusting in what seemed like a foreign environment, I was also challenged with reclaiming and achieving personal, medical, financial, and legal objectives. It took five months of hard work, but I was as able to meet the challenges as well as establish a solid career plan. I felt the Lord leading me to go back to school. So I began my quest to enter college.

I had not been in an academic setting since 1991 where I earned my certification in hotel/motel management. But college was a different ball game, and I hadn't been in a rigorous academic setting since graduating from high school in 1968. It was not difficult to call on God regularly because I knew I needed God's help to take such a big step. Tackling school was a good opportunity to apply my faith, new coping skills and Christ-like discipline and draw on the power of the Holy Spirit. I had just finished six years at "State Prison University" and graduated with honors by being a model prisoner. I had relied on God during that time, and was eager to trust him even more as I expanded my mind academically, just as I had expanded my spirituality.

My plan for the future in order, it was now time for me to spend my days reaching toward those things God had prepared for me. This required research, completing applications and test taking. My initial goal was to earn a certification to be a chemical dependency counselor; however after entering college, my thirst to expand my knowledge expanded and I sought my associate's degree.

The road was not easy. After researching several accredited colleges, I applied to Cleveland State University, and was rejected. Unlike the past, I now understood that rejection is a stepping stone. I accepted it and used it as a source of motivation. I was accepted into Cuyahoga Community College and entered in January of 2001. Going to Cuyahoga turned out to be a true blessing. It was cheaper financially, closer to home and gave more student support services. Before my release date on August 1, 2000, I had registered for classes, gotten my books, and found a place to live.

I found a home in Cleveland, thanks to Mr. Barrett who referred me to a Christian transitional housing facility, Emmanuel Promise of Hope. However, prison policy required inmates to reside in the town where they lived prior to the crime for ninety days. So, I had to return to Youngstown. I really wasn't ecstatic about returning to Youngstown. God had delivered me from that barren, depressing, and desolate place. For me, Youngstown was a step backward, a return to the place of my sin, where a dark cloud hung over me. This scripture came to mind *"As a dog returneth to his vomit, so a fool returneth to his folly" (Proverbs 26:11 KJV).* I had learned in recovery meetings that it was unwise to return to the people, places and things that represented my past life. But the law was the law.

My eldest son and his fiancée picked me up and took me back to Youngstown. Being released felt like another mission accomplished, even though the journey was not complete. I lived with my son for ninety days. I used the time to apply in the secular world the spiritual principles I had learned in prison. These including displaying the attributes of a loving, forgiving, and merciful God sharing my testimony, exhibiting discipline, obedience, and maintaining a made up mind. These were the catalysts for change, and would continue to be. I used every aspect of these qualities during my stay in Youngstown, especially forgiveness from all that had happened in the past.

I felt as though I was on a giant TV screen, with all eyes and ears watching me and listening to my every word. They did not comprehend that I was not concerned about pleasing people but only wanted to do what was right in God's sight. I was not ashamed of letting everyone know that I was not my own anymore, but my heart now belonged to Jesus Christ. I knew the word spoke of *"For whosoever shall be ashamed of me and my words, of him shall the Son of man be ashamed, when he come in his glory, and in his Father's and of the holy angels" (Luke 9:6 KJV).* I was aHoly Ghost-filled prisoner of righteousness who was on fire for the Lord and thankful for all he'd done for me.

Not by works of righteousness which we have done, but according to his mercy he saved us, by the washing of regeneration, and renewing of the Holy Ghost" (Titus 3:5 KJV).

I could not change the past, but I could forgive myself for all the promises I had made and broken, and forgive others for the wrong they'd done to me. The more I learned to forgive, the more my heart changed. Receiving God's divine forgiveness started a chain reaction of forgiveness in my life. Not only was I forgiven, but I could tap into God's divine power to help me forgive others. This genuine forgiveness I experienced removed the guilt, pain, and shame I had lived with for so long.

The first true test of whether I learned the spiritual principle of forgiveness came when I arrived home from prison. Had I really forgiven her, my mother-in-law? As long as I had not come into direct contact with her, intellectually I believed I had. But was I prepared to exhibit forgiveness when I saw her face-to-face. Would I remember the promise of peace which surpasses all human understanding? Would my spiritual maturity be manifested in that moment? Was the new me ready? I asked these questions of myself and God.

This encounter came the first week I was home after I had made arrangements to pick up my children from my mother-in-law's house. Truthfully, my intentions were to avoid her, but when my daughter came out she said her grandma wanted me to come in. I had been sitting in the car praying to God about what would happen during the encounter. I knew He was with me. This was my opportunity to show that I had been transformed by the renewing of my mind, as Paul said in Romans 12: 2. I took a couple of deep breaths, got out of the car and walked towards the front door.

I was very excited to see my children. After sharing hugs, we proceeded to the living room where Grandma sat. I spoke with optimism in my voice believing we would have a good conversation. And, we did. It must have been obvious to her from my manner that I had no animosity towards her. While I'd been incarcerated, I had asked God to teach me forgiveness, and it was during that conversation with my mother-in-law that I knew my prayers had been answered. But I also knew that this was one of many tests, and that my Christian walk and spiritual healing would carry on for the rest of my life.

I had ninety days to reside in Youngstown, and I was determined to make each one of them productive. Taking advantage of every opportunity, tying up every loose end and gathering everything I needed to move to the next phase was my goal.

I met with my parole officer two days after my arrival and he ordered me to attend AA meetings once a week. I humbled myself and complied but also conveyed my desire to leave the city in ninety days in order to establish a new residence, life and education. Initially, he had a negative reaction until I reminded him the parole provision which allowed me to move after ninety days. I visited him two more times before he reassigned me to the Cleveland district office.

During my ninety days in Youngstown, I visited my bishop/pastor, church family and biological family. Fellowshipping and reminiscing with my bishop and spiritual advisor was high on my list of things to do, and I approached with great anticipation. I was anxious to exchange what I learned as a result of my six and a half years of biblical study to Bishop. I wanted to discuss with him the ways my mind had been transformed.

I continued to be tested during my ninety days. One area of testing which surprised me was being exposed to technology. My son had a computer in his apartment which both intrigued and intimidated me. I knew we were in the day and age when I would be required to become technologically savvy in order to be successful in achieving my academic goals. I wondered if I would be able to successfully navigate this unfamiliar path. I believe these doubts were the enemy's way of thwarting my academic plans. But, the word of God continued to be my source of strength. *"And he saith unto them, why are ye fearful, o ye of little faith?" (Matthew 8:26a KJV).* I would not panic during this storm like the disciples did on the boat. *"Behold he that keepeth Israel shall neither slumber nor sleep" (Psalm 121:4 KJV).* I was ready to "get out of the boat." I was ready to completely unpack my old way of thinking and begin life anew. *"Behold, I will do a new thing; now it shall spring forth; shall ye know it?" (Isaiah 43:19a KJV). "Old things are passed away; behold, all things are become new" (2 Corinthians 5:17 KJV).* If I could confront the small things victoriously, I could conquer the big things it would take time, but with God as my guide, I could make it through. I was determined to make the most out of each day, to enjoy it and be productive. God's word says,*"Redeeming the time, because the days are evil" (Ephesians 5: 16 NIV) "Walk in wisdom toward them that are without, redeeming the time" (Colossians 4: 5 KJV).* I studied these and other scriptures daily. I began to set priorities and to engage in activities that were conducive to my well-being and quality of life. I use the gift of the present (today) and live it as if it was my last because tomorrow's not promised. *"Again, he limiteth a certain day, saying in David, today, after so long a time" (Hebrews 4:7 KJV).* Before I was reconciled to God, I had wasted a lot of time acting irresponsibly, and being unappreciative and unreceptive to my God-given life. I had spent much of my life living without God, which is no life at all. I was determined to not waste the rest of the time I was given.

After my ninety days in Youngstown was up, I moved back to Cleveland. I moved into the Emmanuel Promise of Hope facility which I had arranged when I first got paroled. Though I was not thrilled of having to share my living quarters with a group of men (felt like prison), I humbly understood that each step was a step in the right direction. This step represented another ray of light in the direction of complete freedom.

Moving to the Emmanuel House was beneficial in a number of ways. It was close to multiple amenities, downtown, college; the rent was affordable and the house was Christ-centered. When I moved in and got to know the founders, Mr. and Mrs. Buford, I immediately discerned that their spirits illuminated the Holy Spirit, and that God was very present in their lives. I felt accepted and at home immediately. I took the next ten days to get familiar with my new *holding pattern*. College classes would begin early January, so it is vital that I get acquainted with bus routes, the layout of downtown, and my new living companions.

The facility was composed of two large newly refurbished homes located in the back of the founder's home, which made keeping an eye on residents easily. There was a large women's home directly across the street and another home adjacent to the Buford's. The homes were newly furnished and divided into single and double rooms. The area was nice and relatively quiet, and could house up to 26 residents. I lived there for three years until I attained my associate's degree in Human Services.

Soon after arrival, I became a facilitator for EPOH sin, alcohol, tobacco, and other drug support ministry. These groups were held twice per week and were open to all. It was an indispensable Christian support system, one that built up, edified, and encouraged those in recovery. We followed the scriptural mandate which says, ***"Wherefore comfort yourselves together, and edify one another even as also ye do" (1 Thessalonians 5:11 KJV).*** In addition to facilitating this recovery group, I also became a volunteer intake counselor at the City Mission where Mr. Buford worked. In addition to that, being a full-time student and preaching at the City Mission on occasions, my discipline of obedience was paying off. I was taking back everything I'd allowed the devil to take from me.

My first year as full-time student was especially challenging. I was enrolled in prerequisite classes like math, english and science. God's grace and mercy abounded as the Lord placed people to assist me. These included tutors, student services, and a special coach, who had her master's degree, who instructed me in study skills, overcoming obstacles and finding educational grants.

On one occasion during my first semester, I went to my coach because I was thrilled to have received a "C" on a test. She told me that I should strive for nothing less than A's. From that point on, I always strived to reach the highest level. I began to put the same whole-hearted discipline and obedience in my academics as required to be a born-again Christian. I realized that it was just as important for me to seek perfection here on earth as it was in striving toward heaven. As a result of her teaching, I began working harder and achieved Cum Laude, exceptionally high grade point average and made the dean's list. It was difficult, but so is gaining

Jesus and Jesus' deep spiritual truth. I approached my academic lessons with the same vigor as I had spiritual growth. I was now lining up every aspect of life with God's Word. I had come to realizethat anything worth having in life would elude me, if I didn't work diligently to achieve it.

During the first year of school, I took care of some additional life matters, such as filing for divorce, eliminating past debt, and setting up a collaborative outreach network between The City Mission and Bethel Lighthouse Ministries, my home church.

January, 2002 marked the beginning of my second year of college, a year where all was well with my soul though a plethora of events occurred to cause a spiritual and intellectual explosion. My divorce became final. I began a 525 hour internship at the City Mission; and I was invited to numerous motivational speaking engagements. I was ordained in my church and I went to Columbus, Ohio to attain my Minister'slicense. I began taking men from the City Mission on my preaching dates to Youngstown along with my other practicum and volunteer duties.

On one occasion, my cousin asked me to ride to Rochester, New York to visit his mother who was in the hospital having been diagnosed with Alzheimer's disease. I made arrangements to go, especially since I loved my aunt dearly though I hadn't seen her in many years. The visit was good, but because of her illness, she had lost all cognitive functioning, including her ability to communicate. Despite that, when I stood over her and held her hands, I knew in my heart that our spirits connected and she was going to be alright. God spoke to me in his still gentle voice, saying "I got her, she is alright."When we returned to the house, my uncle asked if I was looking for a car. I responded, "Uncle, I did not come up to Rochester, New York to look for a car, I came to see our family." But the Holy Spirit urged me to take a look. In his garage, were his antique classic Lincoln, and Buick Riviera and a white Mark V, the car he was offering me? I asked him how much he wanted for it, and he quoted me a price I couldn't refuse. He also gave me the option to drive the car back to Ohio, and to send him the money in the mail. During the drive back to Ohio, I fell in love with the car. Just as soon as I got back, I mailed the check. It was a great car which needed only minor repairs. I thanked God for this wonderful blessing.

On the March 10, 2002, my spiritual advisor passed away. I was grateful that I had one last visit with him. I also lost a number of relatives including an aunt, soon followed by an uncle who died within days of each other. I also lost my uncle in Rochester, the one who sold me the car. It was definitely, a season of losses. But God be the Glory.

I was in a much better space spiritually than I had been when I had experienced other losses.

It is better to go to the house of mourning, than to go to the house of feasting: for that is the end of all men; and the living will lay it to his heart." (Ecclesiastes 2:4 KJV). The heart of the wise is in the house of mourning; but the heart of fools is in the house of mirth." (Ecclesiastes 7:2,4 KJV).

When my uncle died, my aunt called to ask if I would do the eulogy. Honored, I accepted the invitation to perform my first eulogy. I felt overwhelmed, but I knew it was my calling and God would see me through. I immediately called my pastor who provided his usual dose of support and guidance. I was comforted by his presence and felt confident and began preparing.

I spent two and a half days in Youngstown visiting, asking relevant questions so that I could meet the new challenge of helping to celebrate my uncle's life. The funeral was significant not only because I loved my uncle, but because it was yet another phase in my rebirth. During the process, I gained confidence and was reassured that this was my calling. I also learned many things such as order, empathy, and sensitivity. When it was all over, I received many comments that confirmed my calling. Also the answers to questions I posed to my Bishop, helped me to learn and grow in my ability to help others.

Before I accepted Jesus as my Lord and Savior, I was uncomfortable with death, funerals, and losses in general. I had not handled death well, but this loss, was different I had helped others in the process. This was just another sign that my old self was being transformed. *"For which cause we faint not; but though our outward man perish, yet the inward man is renewed day by day." (2 Corinthians 4:16 KJV).*

Since my transformation, I had operated mostly in the spiritual realm. So much so, my college coach asked if I knew how to be human. After processing her question, I had to admit that I really did not. I had to consider whether the way I communicated and behaved was appropriate. My renewed mind aligned scripturally butI was feeling like I was living in a strange land. During my time in prison, I had spent my time studying to show myself approved *"unto God, a workman that needeth not be ashamed, rightly dividing the word of truth" (2 Timothy 2: 15 KJV).* But I hadn't really learned to stop to smell the roses. I had to learn how to be human again and acclimate to society.

Overcoming the losses, did not get in the way of my working passionately for my full freedom from the judicial system. I was overjoyed to be paroled and enjoyed the new freedoms it allowed. The level of joy I experienced was something I'd never felt before. I don't remember at what point Satan had stolen my joy, smile, and life because it happened bit by bit. But this I know, God gave my freedom back on January 4, 2002. *"If the son therefore shall make you free, ye shall be free indeed." (John 8:36 KJV).* For the first time, I was feeling completely free in mind, body, and soul. Hallelujah! I was whole again, no longer a broken cistern. I had found spiritual fulfillment. Apart from God, I could not have imagined what it feels like to be free. I was definitely able to have more positive day to day experiences as well as manage bad feelings through the power of the Holy Spirit. Feelings only last for a moment. God was allowing His divine nature to permeate my soul and personality. This new found joy would continue to bear fruit in my life.

"But the fruits of the Spirit is love, peace, longsuffering, gentleness, goodness, faith, meekness, temperance (Galatians 5:222,23a KJV). But they that wait upon the Lord shall renew their strength; they shall mount up with wings as eagles" (Isaiah 40:31 KJV).

The year 2003 had it challenges, but God's divine grace was ever present and His promises remained true. School was becoming more challenging and I had not yet mastered test anxiety. I was determined not to let these small obstacles overtake me. The Word of God empowered me. I found myself needing Him more and more, needing Jesus incessantly. If I didn't know anything else, I knew I could call on the Lord. Because I wanted something I had never had, I had to do something I'd never done. I had to use radical methods in seeking God's guidance and scholarly knowledge. Until I allowed Jesus to be my master and liberator, I was unreachable as well as unteachable. But God had now become a part of my life's journey, including the journey through school. **"And whatsoever ye do, do it heartily, as to the Lord, and not unto men" (Colossians 3:23 KJV).**

In 2003, it was not without its share of losses. On February 3, 2003, my friend, Captain McKay, went home to be with the Lord. I also lost my cousin, a highly regarded police officer, in Rochester, New York on February 28, 2003. Then his mother died in June. These losses enhanced my faith and I was determined to keep my mind stayed on Jesus.

Graduation was now in sight. I realized that I needed to better position myself for what was beyond my associate's degree. One of my challenges was to become computer literate. To date, I had paid individuals to type my papers. I had tried to learn the in's and out's of using the computer; including taking classes, but was not very successful. Finally, I decided to buy a computer of my own. By year's end through prayer, countless errors, phone calls, and technical support, I had made significant progress.

Having better computer skills influenced my decision to pursue a bachelor's degree in Social Work. Through my studies, I began understanding the needs and perspectives of the less fortunate. I believed a social work degree would give me the skills to work with diverse populations. I also believed such a degree would pair well with ministry, as Christian communities have always played a significant role in serving needy, lonely, disabled, elderly and grieving people. I was also open to the idea that further study would allow me to fulfill my own need for counseling to sort out my issues.

"For thou hast been a strength to the poor, a strength to the needy in his distress (Isaiah 25:4a KJV).

I had compassion for people and this work. In my heart, I wanted to be the best I could be. I understood my need to be educated, well rounded, and strengthened in all aspects of my being. I was still on the potter's wheel. God was molding, shaping, and chiseling me into a new creation. *"Therefore if any man be in Christ, he is a new creature: old things are passed away; behold, all things are become new"* (2 Corinthians 5:17 KJV). With this molding came suffering. But I was actually encountering a new kind of suffering. You see, there is a distinct difference from suffering doing evil and suffering doing what's right in God's sight. *"I am crucified with Christ: nevertheless I live; yet not I, but Christ liveth in me: and the life which I now live in the flesh I live by the faith of the Son of God, who loved me and gave himself for me." (Galatians 2: 20 KJV). "Beloved think it not strange concerning the fiery trial which is to try you, as though some strange thing happened unto you: but, rejoice, inasmuch as ye are partakers of Christ's sufferings; that, when his glory shall be revealed, ye may be glad also with exceeding joy" (1 Peter 4:12,13 KJV).*

All the struggles paid off, and on May 15, 2003, I graduated. Relatives and friends joined me in celebrating this milestone. And even though I was fifty-four years old, I couldn't have been happier if I had been twenty-four.*"But they that wait upon the Lord shall renew their strength; they shall mount up with wings as eagles; they shall run and not be weary; and they shall walk and not faint." (Isaiah 40:31 KJV).*

After graduation, I entered a four year college and accepted other new challenges and positions. I became a volunteer chaplain at Crossroads, our Men's Ministry at The City Mission. I had multiple duties, butI enjoyed family counseling most because it allowed me to gain insight into the various present issues that the residents had. It also, helped me further my healing process. I went on to become vice president of the board of director of EPOH, the transitional facility where I had lived while on parole. In this position, I acquired valuable knowledge on how boards work. Everything that was going on in my life continued to line up with scripture, *"The wind bloweth whereit listeth, and thou hearest the sound thereof, but can not tell whence it cometh, and whither it goeth: so is every one that is born of the spirit" (John 3:8 KJV).* These positions allowed me to expand my professional network and experience. God had placed me in these voluntary positions so that I could learn, give back, and redevelop. God had freed me so I could help liberate others. *"Brethern, if a man be overtaken in a fault, ye which are spiritual, restore an one in the spirit of meekness; considering thyself, lest thou also be tempted. Bear ye one another's burdens, and so fulfill the law of Christ. For if a man think himself to be something when he is nothing, he deceiveth himself. But let every man prove his own work, and then shall he have rejoicing in himself alone, and not in another., For every man shall bear his own burden"(Galatians 6:1-5 KJV).*

"Consider it pure joy, my brothers, whenever you face trials of many kinds, because you know that the testing of your faith develops perseverance. Perseverance must finish its work so that you may be mature and complete, not lacking anything" (James 1: 1-4 NIV).

Getting into a four year college was pretty intense. It is significantly more challenging than community college. The first university that accepted me was too expensive. So, I had to search for one that was more suitable to my financial situation. Then there was the challenge of having a felony conviction which required me to go through additional hurdles to prove that I was credit-worthy. I was required to submit written statements about my conviction and incarceration. I was not going to allow my past to determine my future. I was not going to allow others to box me in because of my past mistakes. The following is an excerpt from a letter I wrote to a college board in response to questions about my felony conviction and my worthiness to enroll in their school.

Dear Board Members:

Should a man be judged twice for his past? Should a man be vilified again and again? Even when he has done a 180 degree turn after dealing with his jealousy? Even after he has paid in full his dues for the wrong? **"Therefore if any man be in Christ, he is a new creature: old things are passed away;behold, all things are become new" (2 Corinthians 5: 17 KJV).** *In addition,* **"For with what judgment ye judge, ye shall be judged: and with what measure ye mete, it shall be measured to you again" (Matthew 7:2 KJV).** *Dear Board Members* **"Let us not therefore judge one another anymore: but judge this rather, that no man put a stumblingblock or an** occasion to fall in his brother's way" (Romans 14: 13 KJV)."**For if ye forgive men their trespasses, your heavenly Father will also forgive you: But if ye forgive not men their trespasses, neither will your Father forgive your trespasses" (Matthew 6:14,15 KJV).** *Finally Sirs and Madams,* **"Withhold not good from them to whom it is due, when it is in the power of thine hand to do it" (Proverbs 3: 27 KJV).** *To my understanding of your Educational Department Mission Statement, I qualify unequivocally.* **The unit's mission is to prepare competent, caring, committed professionals to teach, lead and serve diverse communities of learners.**

I tried to convey to this Evangelical Christian Lutheran College that if they did not admit me, another college would. Through God's grace and my persistence, I was accepted. Years later, I would use this same letter to gain admittance into Ashland Theological Seminary for my master's degree, and to obtain my licensure from the National Association of Social Workers **"And we know that all things work together for good to them that love God, to them who are called according to his purpose" (Romans 8:28 KJV).**

During this year, I was able to fly to Las Vegas to meet my brother and visit our uncle. It had been over ten years since we had seen each other. He drove across the desert from Mesa, Arizona, and we visited for three days. Like me, he too had overcome drug and alcohol addiction. We talked about our struggles, family, shared memories and future goals. The visit allowed us to bond, communicate soberly, and experience brotherly love. We also spent time with our uncle in Las Vegas who was ill. It felt like old times. When the visit was over, we went away encouraged, enlightened, and jovial. This would be the last time I would see either one of them again.

After returning back to school, I began fulfilling my practicum hours at a dual geriatric facility. I worked in two buildings one housed patients who were mobile and could meet some of their own needs; the other side served more critically ill patients who had greater physical and mental challenges. I saw first hand how residents were being mistreated, over medicated, and neglected. When I brought these issues to the attention of the director, the facility actually made great strides to resolve the many issues. During this internship, I improved my ability to advocate for others, developed empathy, gained knowledge of diverse cultures, as well as spiritual sensitivity and awareness. I also gained the respect of the administrators, nurses, families and the residents. I left the internship feeling super about the progress I had made and the impact I had left.

In contrast to this success, in mid-August, I hit a rough spot. One of the men I had counseled for a little over a year at The City Mission, passed away after a serious illness. I was the only counselor who was willing to take this young man's case because he had so many issues. I did not see him as a leper as some of my colleagues did. He was someone who needed my help, and I was determined to help him.

When he died, the young man's oldest brother, asked me to help plan and officiate his home going service. I was gratified to know that this young man respected me and my style of ministering. I gladly accepted the calling since I had been a large part of his life and the life of his son and his son's mother for the past year. As usual, I sought the guidance and support of my Bishop/Pastor. I was grateful to God for the large attendance and support. The Holy Spirit enabled, empowered, and made all things possible.

In November, I got a call from my cousin in Youngstown to say that his dad, my uncle had died. My schedule would not permit me to attend the funeral, but I emphasize this loss because like other recent losses, my new man was able to handle losses in ways that were not destructive to me, others or my relationship with God. Had I not made the choice to change, I would have remained unhealthy and the blessings of life would have passed me by. I was only able to change with Jesus' help. He assisted me in turning defeat into victory, sadness into gladness, and hopelessness into being more than a conqueror.**"Because they have no changes, therefore they fear not God." (Psalm 55:19b KJV).** If one is not moving and continuously changing, then one is dying and already dead spiritually. **"For if ye thoroughly amen your ways and your doings; if ye thoroughly execute judgment between a man and his neighbor; if ye oppress not the stranger, the fatherless, and the widow, and shed not innocent blood in this place, neither walk after other gods to your hurt: then will I cause you to dwell in this place, in the land that I gave to your fathers, forever and ever. Behold, ye trust in lying words that cannot profit. (Jeremiah 7:5-8 KJV).**

During my continuous process of change, I would acquire greater knowledge and a reverence for God. In 2005, I received a fresh infusion of faith through devout study of spiritual and scholarly matters. I read a variety of books. Some of the reading was soft, other readings of the books werehard causing me to discern and resist things that did not line up biblically. For school, I was required to read an assortment of books on cognitive behavioral theories, human development, psychology perspectives and counseling therapeutic techniques.

One of the most challenging but interesting reading was Richard Tarnas'book titled, *The Passion of the Western Mind*. I was so enthralled with the philosophers and their world perspectives; I could discern who believed in God and who doubted. I could relate to and understand my new worldview, psyche, and creator of my cosmos even more than I had before. This study led to the conclusion I needed, I would continue my education in seminary. There, I would be able to integrate biblical approaches with cognitive, behavioral, existential, and other therapeutic approaches. I understood that it was essential for me to attain education that would allow me to translate psychological terms for use as a Christian or biblical counselor. I wanted to be able to express myself in theological and psychological communities.

Knowing that I wanted my education to continue, I worked extremely hard that year to keep my grade point average high. This would improve my chances of getting into school and obtaining scholarships and other financial aid. I was well into my journey of making new choices, to become better not bitter.

Wherefore, *"God hath dealt to every man the measure of faith"* (general knowledge) *(Romans 12: 3 KJV)*. But *"even so faith, if it hath not works, is dead, being alone" (James 2:17 KJV)*. Faith pushes, moves us, and prompts us and will not let evil harm us (protects). *"For whatever is born of God overcometh the world and this is the victory that has overcometh the world even our faith" (1John 5:4, 5 KJV)*. Faith is powerful and unstoppable *"because the one who in you is."* In addition to experiencial spiritual healing and growth, my self-confidence and confidence in Jesus also grew. I had a *more than a conqueror* faith, an overcomer's mentality, and saving grace in my heart. With His word hidden in my heart and a year away from graduation, my feelings could best be expressed in the words of the prophet Jeremiah,*"Ah Lord God! behold, thou hast made the heaven and the earth by thy great power and stretched out arm, and there is nothing too hard for thee" (Jeremiah 32:17 KJV).*

Life continued to hand me losses. In August of 2004, I received a call from my Auntie that my Uncle from Las Vegas had died. *"However no one knows the day or the hour, not even the angels in heaven, or the son himself, but only the Father" (Matthew 24:36 KJV).* Every one of my losses today was different than yesterday. Today I understand *"And as it is appointed unto men once to die, but after this the judgment." (Hebrews 9: 27 KJV).* Death is a reality. We live to die but Jesus gives eternal life.*"He that believeth on the son hat everlasting life: and he that believeth not the Son shall not see life; but the wrath of God abideth on him: (John 3:36 KJV).* I gained comfort in knowing my meaning, purpose, and final destination was to be with Jesus. I no longer feared dying. *"And deliver them who through fear of death were all their lifetime subject to bondage" (Hebrews 2:15 KJV).*

As 2006 entered, *"I press toward the mark for the prize of the high calling of God in Christ Jesus" (Philippians 3:14 KJV).* Obedience and discipline were not only evidence of faith, but necessary for my quality of life. I needed them both for physical, spiritual, and emotional health. I needed them for self-care, self-management, and daily life. Though the world was not getting any better, to God be the glory, I was. I have come to learn that life is just life. Empowered by the Holy Spirit, I react, respond, and reply differently to life's challenges with a Christ-like attitude *"Let no man deceive you with vain words: for because of these things cometh the wrath of God upon the children of disobedience" and "see then that ye walk circumspectly, not as fools, but as wise, but understanding what the will of the Lord is" (Ephesians 5:6, 15-17 KJV).* Christians are not exempt from life's daily tribulations, temptations, trials, afflictions, and suffering. We simply rely on God to see us through.

"Rejoicing in hope, patient in tribulation, continuing instant in prayer" (Romans 12:12 KJV).

"There hath no temptation taken you but such as is common to man: but God is faithful, who will not suffer you to be tempted above that ye are able; but will with the temptation also make a way to escape, that ye may be able to bear it" (1 Corinthians10:13 KJV).

"Beloved, think it not strange concerning the fiery trial which is to try you, as though some strange thing happened unto you" (1 Peter 4:12 KJV).

"And not only so, but we glory in tribulations also: knowing that tribulation workethpatience" (Romans 5:3 KJV).

The year 2006 was a year of immense studying, exposure, and learning to regulate personal emotions, and prepare for Theological training in other areas. These tools would prepare me for a major in pastoral counseling. I added to the array of knowledge I had acquired more biblical tools needed for my calling to a ministry of encouragement and comfort. Through the grace of God, I received a bachelor's degree in social work in August, 2006 with honors. Many more of my family members attended graduation which brought me great joy. After graduation, I focused on getting into Ashland Theological Seminary. While I still had to endure extra scrutiny due to my past, my G.P.A was very high and I had lived a life that was above reproach. More importantly, Jesus had promised and assured me *"I can do all things through Christ which strengtheneth me." (Philippians 4:13 KJV).*

In my heart, I prayed that my three teenagers and my granddaughter would be encouraged to get their education. I had done something for me and I was heading for my master's. I was also convinced that a doctorate was within reach now. Like Joseph in the bible, I was now dreaming big dreams.

Also during this year, my cousin whom led me to the Lord Jesus Christ entered into eternal rest on November 4, 2006. That was another substantial loss for me which only strengthened me and encouraged me to stay fixated on the Lord. His wife asked me to participate in the service, and I agreed. The home going celebration uplifted me in so many ways. I saw many family and friends that I otherwise would not have seen. I stood before the world as a sign that God lives and that God is good. I was preparing to do what God wanted me to do rather than what I chose to do, all to God be the Glory.

Then came 2007, which would be a year of turning points and transitions. Turning points and transitions are simply curves that take one off the main path into unknown territory. Although the year would be exciting, interesting, traumatic, and even life threatening, God was always near. His promise is true: *"I will never leave thee, nor forsake thee" (Hebrews 13:5 KJV).* I had already found in God's word the stability which flowed through me and gave me reassurance of Godly character.

"I am the vine; ye are the branches: He that abideth in me, and I in him, the same bringeth forth much fruit: for without me ye can do nothing" *(John 15:5 KJV).* I wanted to know all I could about God's importance of human relationships and dignity of worth of individuals. *"For God so loved the world that he gave his only begotten son" (John 3:16 KJV).* Studying the bible was one of my favorite activities. The Old Testament piqued my interest immensely, specifically the prophesies of Jesus' coming. I was in awe of the good kings, bad kings as well as the major and minor prophets. I was dismayed by the Israelites' continuous disobedience and their plight to constantly do what was right in their own sight. But, more interestingly for me was how God through His love and outstretched hands incessantly displayed His love, compassion, and mercy towards them. It was interesting to learn the Israelites' general patterns of movement. I was also intrigued with the bible as literary works written in three original languages of Hebrew, Aramaic, and Greek. I pursued an understanding of hermeneutics, all of its complexities and uniqueness were challenging to me. I came to recognize the process of learning about the bible was never ending. Studying the word was a way of reading then rereading, studying and interpreting were essential to my spiritual growth. Seminary classes would help me in the exegesis, application, hermeneutic, and contextual writing of sermons. I believed personal interaction when reading God's Word sanctioned our relationship. *"But there is a spirit in man: and the inspiration of the almighty giveth them understanding" (Job 31:8 KJV).* Attempting to understand such courses of empirical and scientific understanding without God had no substance. *"But the comforter which is the hold ghost, whom the Father will send in my name, he shall teach you all things, and bring all things to your remembrance, whatsoever I have*

said unto you" (John 14:26 KJV). Studying a range of meanings constantly led me into a spiritual realm. No wonder God said,*"All scripture is given by inspiration of God, and is profitable for doctrine, for reproof, for correction, for instruction in righteousness" (2Timothy 3:16 KJV).* The genre and sub-genre and theological re-description of reality also interested me. The biblical lexicon in all its variety of languages held my interest and made school exciting.

The excitement of school was dampened by health concerns which arose. Generally, I can determine when my body is going through changes. In retrospect, I should have known in 2006 that something was toxic to my physical body. I ignored what was going on because I was determined to graduate on time. I was so centered on school that I refused to recognize that I was suffering under the spirit of infirmity. I also knew in my heart and kept in my prayer this profound scripture. *"No weapon that is formed against thee shall prosper; and every tongue that shall rise against thee in judgment thou shalt condemn" (Isaiah 54:17a,b KJV).*

When June came, I started my four summer courses. This was the heaviest summer load I had ever taken. I was determined to finish what I started. I did begin to notice that I would become fatigued and that rest did not solve the problem. Though I noticed certain physical changes such as itching, swelling of my ankles, and even the slight yellowing in my eye color, I refused to acknowledge them. I thought this too shall past. After much hashing over in my mind, I decided to drop a class which appeared to be overwhelming. I ended the summer term with two A's and a B.

Immediately after summer classes ended, I went to a doctor to get checked out. He told me that there might be a problem with my liver. Unhappy with this doctor because he had to confer with another specialist, I switched doctors. The following week, I was diagnosed with severe cirrhosis of the liver. This explained the symptoms I had been feeling for months. The symptoms became unbearable. I could not even adorn a cotton t-shirt, had no teardrops, or wax in my ears. I was messed up and I did not understand what was happening to my body nor could I explain it to others. I was bombarded with questions like, how, when, where did you get it. I isolated myself from others but drew closer to the only one who knew me and the situation, Jesus. Faced with another brush with death, I was in denial. Nevertheless, I knew Jesus,*"He shall not be afraid of evil tidings: his heart is fixed, trusting in the Lord" (Psalm 112:7 KJV).*

The second week of August, I was presented with an option to get on the liver recipient list. I did not want to have a transplant because doctors said the surgery was eight to nine hours long. The survival rate was suspect, and I would possibly have to take rejection medicines the rest of my life. Besides, there were 147 people ahead of me on the list. I was in intense discussion with Jesus about how much pain and discomfort I had already been through. I got a phone call from an unknown woman trying to sell me something. When I mentioned the liver transplant, she told me she'd had one three years ago and was doing fine. She assured me that with modern technology and it's a much simpler procedure today. That conversation caused me to rethink my decision not to get the transplant. Later that night while laying bedside, I heard once again that still, small voice say,"My child have I not been with you through it all even when you were in your mess." Hallelujah! I popped up like toast and began praising and thanking Jesus. He had not brought me this far to leave me.

At the end of August I decided to take a mini vacation or get away. Supernaturally, I got a phone call from the transplant team nurse seeking additional information. After providing her the information, I told her I was headed out of town. She told me I needed to stay close if they needed to locate me. I didn't really take to heart what she'd said. Instead I went on with my daily routine. I was now processing life or death issues and focusing on finishing school.

On August 31, 2007 as I lay sleep, I received a phone call at 3:30 a.m. summoning me to the hospital. My new liver or what I like to think of as God's liver for me was available and I needed to get to the hospital immediately. I couldn't believe it. I even asked if I could finish sleeping and be there at 10:00 a.m. The caller made it plain that I needed to act now, so I agreed and hung up. As I arose with tears in my eyes and started praying to God for confirmation, comfort, and strength, it was only God because I had not even been on the list for three weeks.

After prayer and crying, I called my cousin and her husband to share the news being a wise woman of God, though not completely understanding what I had just self-disclosed, my cousin encouraged me to get ready. They picked me up. I became emotional again when I explained that a liver was available. After sharing with them how I'd wrestled with the decision to have the surgery, my cousin's husband told me, "You better go get God's liver." Her husband, his statement confirmed for me to go ahead and have surgery.

Two hours later, I was being prepped for surgery. I awoke in the hospital after a 9 hour surgery, grateful to see the light of another day. I was cut from top of my chest downward and across from rib cage to rib cage. There were tubes everywhere. AlthoughI had been cut, poked and probed in the strangest places, I knew I would live on. *"I shall not die, but live and declare the works of the Lord" (Psalm 118:17 KJV).* I knew God was in the equation.*"The Lord preserve thy going out and thy coming in from this time forth, and even forever more" (Psalm 121:8 KJV).*

I was released on the 13th of September, on my way home to fully recover. Recovery took much prayer, physical therapy, and unadulterated faith. The two most astounding supernatural occurrences happened during this process."Hallelujah"My testimony is *"Come and hear, all ye that fear God¸ and I will declare what he hath done for my soul" (Psalm 66:16 KJV).* I finished the year in good health and immensely thankful that I could continue my mind-blowing journey.

The year 2008 came in. Graduation was nearing. I ensured some challenging mid-terms and finals in conjunction with preparation for licensure. I reduced some of my other obligations due to my health, but kept God, me and school in the forefront. Self-care, spiritual maintenance, and priorities have been rearranged through forgiveness, obedience, and discipline learned by God's word. I will be forever grateful to God for allowing me the freedom to improve my position through forgiveness. Forgiveness made me willing to dissipate all the disruptive and destructive patterns of thought and behavior.

Educational and medical debt has left me in a financial quandary, so I chose not to pursue my doctorate, although I had my thesis pretty much outlined. Being the first in the Harris family to attain a master's degree would have to suffice. Getting a doctorate would show my children what they could achieve. I also wanted to leave them Godly traits, employability skills, personal values, the critical tools needed to succeed in life. I have set the bar high. I wanted my kindred to be under the tutelage of the Holy Spirit which is paramount. God has given the believer, *"all things that pertain unto life and godliness" (2Peter 2:3).* The Holy Spirit, who indwells us, is the spirit of truth," anything else is dishonesty and counterfeit. I wanted my family knowledgeable to accepting God's WORD as truth which would allow them to discern and ascertain truth. What is truth in secular education, books, and all other aspects of life is revealed through the word of God. *"If ye continue in my word, then are ye my disciples indeed; and ye shall know the truth, and the truth shall make you free" (John 8:31,32 KJV).* The Bible conveys, *"For we can do nothing against the truth, but for the truth" (2 Corinthians 13:2 KJV).* I also wanted to show my family that finding meaning and purpose regardless the situation, can be accomplished through forgiveness, discipline, and obedience. In spite of the afflictions and discouragements internally and externally and even in oppressive circumstances, the dynamics of the process remain the same. *"Wherein ye greatly rejoice, though now for a season, if need be, ye are in heaviness through man, fold temptations: that the trial of your faith, being much more precious than God that perisheth, though it be tried with fire, might be found unto praise and honour and glory at the appearing of Jesus Christ" (1 Peter 1: 6,7 KJV).*

Aunt Doris died on April 13, 2008. I also lost a couple of long time associates. As before, God's Word is where I find solace, refuge, along with strength and peace, joy, and stability. Deaths, remind me that we discover and rediscover Christ. It is an unending process of spiritual growth and development. Where others may have an almost instantaneous crisis conversion, my faith is one that is perpetually evolving.

I received my Master's in Pastoral Counseling (M.P.C.) on December 13, 2008. This milestone would finally allow me to close the door in my past. For the first time, I experienced no residue of shame, guilt, or childhood traumatic events. My emotional problems such as distorted ideas of God, crippling views of self, destructive habits, and hurts from the past were resolved. This change came through the power of genuine forgiveness. This did not mean that the past had left my conscious awareness, but my past had become my past and would only be used to show the goodness of God and to glorify him.

"And they overcame him by the blood of the lamb, and by the word of their testimony; and they loved not their lives unto the death" (Revelation 12:11 KJV).

I would use my past to warn others before they spiraled out of control, help them rethink their position while in the down spiral, or help someone out of the down spiraling. "For we dare not make ourselves of the number, or compare ourselves with some that commend themselves: but they measuring themselves by themselves, and comparing themselves among themselves, are not wise. But we will not boast of things without our measure, but according to the measure of the rule which God hath distributed to us, a measure to reach even unto you. For we stretch not ourselves beyond our measure, as though we reached not unto you: for we are come as far as to you also in preaching the gospel of Christ: Not boasting of things without our measure, that is, of other men's labours; but having hope, when your faith is increased, that we shall be enlarged by you according to our rule abundantly, To preach the gospel in the regions beyond you, and not to boast in another man's line of things made ready to our hand. But he that glorieth, let him glory in the Lord. For not he that commendeth himself is approved, but whom the Lord commendeth. 2 Corinthians 10:12-18 KJV).

Regardless how long, diligent, and spiritually healthy or grounded evil thoughts do not permanently past. I still have to bring or *"And bringing into captivity every thought to the obedience of Christ" (2 Corinthians 10:5b KJV).* I still fall short of the glory of God. I have not arrived. Even though I don't have the proclivity for many things I used to, the sinful thought at times, surfaces. Only now, I do not stay stuck or put myself in situations I know will disrupt my new founded character when simply asking for repentance allows me to carry on. I am no longer spiritually ignorant to Satan's devices nor do I go around deceiving or lying to myself. *"Be not deceived, God is not mocked; for whatsoever a man soweth, that shall he also reap" (Galatians 6: 7 KJV).* Now that I know the truth, I cannot treat God with contempt. God knows, sees, and hears all. It's not like I am still worldly minded when in all actuality, I am now spiritually minded. So it behooves me to sow to the spiritual that I may reap eternal glory. *"Be not deceived: evil communications corrupt good manners" (1Corinthians 15: 33 KJV).* It's a blessing understanding spiritual warfare requires spiritual resources and knowledge of scripture gives one the consciousness to indentify, in union with the power and authority over Satan and diverse temptations.

"My people are destroyed for lack of knowledge; because thou hast rejected knowledge, I will also reject thee, that thou shalt be no priest to me: seeing thou hast forgotten the law of thy God, I will also forget thy " *(Hosea 4:6 KJV).* Finally, consciously mindful that the enemy *"cometh not, but for to steal, and to kill, and to destroy" (John 10:10 KJV)* has me totally persuaded of God's unconditional love. This scripture reminds me how the thief came to steal my life and soul in the past. The scripture expresses how he tried to kill me with worldly and fleshly pleasures. Scripture distinctly reveals how he attempted to destroy my God given meaning and purpose as a true man of God. Yes, I am unequivocally persuaded through His only Son, Jesus' death, burial, and resurrection of God's agape love for me. I'm persuaded to the point in my life *"For I am persuaded that neither death, nor life, nor angels, nor principalities, nor powers, nor things present, nor things to come, nor height, nor depth, nor any creature, shall be able to separate us from the love of God, which is in Christ Jesus our Lord" (Romans 8:38,39 KJV).*

My Life Today: Better Not Bitter

My life today is good only because God is good, good all the time. I have grown and am still growing closer to God; I take life one day at a time scripturally and literally. I live each day by the scripture, *"Wherefore, my beloved, as ye have always obeyed, not as in my presence only, but now much more in my absence, work out your own salvation with fear and trembling. For it is God which worketh in you both to will and to do of his good pleasure. Do all things without murmurings and disputings:That ye may be blameless and harmless, the sons of God, without rebuke, in the midst of a crooked and perverse nation, among whom ye shine as lights in the world;"* (Philippians 2:12-15 KJV). *Today, I am here and have an enthusiastic attitude because of the word of God*"Wherefore (as the Holy Ghost saith, *"To day if ye will hear his voice,*[12] *Take heed, brethren, lest there be in any of you an evil heart of unbelief, in departing from the living God. But exhort one another daily, while it is called To day; lest any of you be hardened through the deceitfulness of sin.(Hebrews 3:7, 12-13 KJV).* For me, the scripture orders my steps, line upon line and precept upon precept, and keeps me rooted and grounded in today. The Bible discloses,*"But he answered and said, it is written, man shall not live by bread along, but by every word that proceedeth out of the mouth of God (Matthew 4:4 KJV).* I hunger daily for my spiritual food *"Give us this day our daily bread" (Matthew 6:11 KJV).* This order leaves me dependent on today.*"Take no thought for the morrow; for the morrow shall take thought for the things of itself. Sufficient unto the day is the evil thereof" (Matthew 6:34 KJV).* This order gives me so much joy because my mind is stayed on,*"This is the day which the Lord has made; we will rejoice and be glad in it" (Psalm 118:24 KJV).*

God continued to bless in 2009 in immeasurable ways. First, God's supernatural power allowed the medical debt of $250,000, I had incurred for the liver transplant operation to be cancelled. Hallelujah! The Lord also allowed me to get rid of my academic financial debt of $94,000. To God be the Glory! I prayed to God about these matters. I do not know how God did, but God did. I do not know the details, but I do know I am a faith individual who *"For we walk by faith, not by sight" (2 Corinthians 5:7 KJV).* I also know *"Now faith is the substance of things hoped for, the evidence of things not seen" (Hebrews 11:1 KJV)."Calleth those things which be not as though they were" (Romans 4:17b KJV)* because I have power to speak positive into my life, believe what I speak, and I trust God to do what he says. Glory!God's favor can be yours too. Just call him up!!! He will *"neither slumber nor sleep" (Psalm 121:4 KJV).* He will never put you on hold and nor is His line busy. Glory!

During 2009, I also experienced a great loss. My brother who was a year younger than I am was hit by a speeding car while riding his bike. He was thrown a good distance, then landed on the pavement when he was marred even more. My two sisters took it hard, and were understandably very angry with the driver. But I chose forgiveness the day I received the report. It was out of my hands; I had no heaven or hell nor did I have the right to judge or distribute prison time.

I needed to be there to support my sisters and bond with them in our time of bereavement. I felt no need to contaminate my mind with toxic information about a young, fatherless, and irresponsible lost kid. If you have trouble envisioning what type of young man this was, just think of today's generation of young men, uneducated, incarcerated, drug obsessed, unaccountable, and unemployed. Include profane babble multiplied by wilderness mentalities; blurred rapper fantasies then subtract all moral restraint. I have been in that epidemic, done time with that culture, and observed how others show no forgiveness. In all actuality, I saw no other option but to forgive this young man whom I never met. God gave me the promise of peace *"which passed all understanding" (Philippians 4: 7 KJV.)* God also promised growth during difficult life experiences, *"He staggered not at the promise of God through unbelief; but was strong in faith, giving glory to God; and being fully persuaded that, what he had promised, he was able also to perform" (Romans 4:20,21 KJV).* While this was a disappointing and horrible event to endure for I truly loved my brother, I understood he was the Lord's and was just on loan to me for God's appointed time. I was comforted by all the lives he touched and the people who loved and said good things about his life's deeds. I was better not bitter. Hallelujah!

Not long after one brother died, I received the shocking news that another one of my brothers had died in Arizona. I wasn't aware of it, but he suffered from kidney and liver ailments. I was unable to make the trip from Georgia to Arizona on such short notice, but thank God my baby sister flew out to represent the family. I was very emotional because I no longer had any living brothers. He and I had been planning to visit each other in Las Vegas soon. Our family was dwindling. My auntie, older and baby sisters and I are the last of the Harris' of that generation. This made the loss of my brother extremely poignant. I wanted to be there to help my sisters in every way possible. It was only through the grace of God that I was able to fill such a privilege and responsibility. I was pleased to be supportive of my family, as well as people from all walks of life, church members and non-church members. In October 1, 2009, I was blessed with the opportunity to move to a warmer climate, Atlanta. I had become health-conscious and believed that my quality of life would improve by living in a warmer climate. I love the South, specifically the weather though I had to get used to allergies due to pollen. I took the first year to get rooted and grounded and assimilate to being a Georgia resident. Mindful that God allotted me this time to strengthen our relationship and to finish this book. Thank You, Jesus! You Alone Are Worthy!

I was led to a great new church home and pastor. I am continuing my prison writing ministry, phone ministry, and waiting for my direction as to which ministry I will assist at church. I still do motivational speaking and preaching when called. I am learning networking, outreaching, social/group networking and all systems relevant to serving the less fortunate in my existing area. I also continue to use my social work skills to advocate for social policies that advance social justice and diversity. God has brought me a long way. My prayer is that God will continue to use me in His service.

A Closing Prayer

"O God, my Creator and Redeemer, I may not go forth today except Thou dost accompany me with Thy blessings. Let not the vigor and freshness of the morning or the glow of good health or the present prosperity of my unknown undertaking deceive me into false reliance upon my own strength.

All these good gifts have come from me from thee. They were thine to give and they are thine to also curtail.

They are not mine to keep. I do not hold them in trust and only in continued dependence upon Thee, the giver, can they be worthily enjoyed. Amen.

Poems

These three poems were written during my long suffering journey:

Thank you, Lord

Jesus, I love you so

You have rescued me from sin

Even secretly and deeply within

You have made me whole

What a complete feeling of being

You have shown me how to be content

Thank you, for the indescribable gift You sent

You have removed my hardened heart

And given me one of flesh

I thank You, Abba Father for these gifts

Now my life is not burdened down with ifs

You have given me a sober and alert mind

Also, with the power to put my old life behind

I thank You, Master for the work you have done

Now my new life has just begun

I thank You for the love through Your Son

Truth is that's when it first begun

Thank you for the peace I now have

And not as the world gives

Lord, I thank You for the joy each precious day

That comes along with following You

Yes, Rabbi, the strength and guidance to

Thank You for the liberty and all so present sanity

I am grateful to You for creating me

Into someone that You can see

Thank You, Lord I no longer walk in daze or maze

That's why now I render You all the praise

You alone are worthy, Father God

Glory to You and Hallelujah.

(January 16, 1996)

Ma, Oh, My Love for You

Ma, even though I have forgiven you

I now understand you were hurt

Wounded, battered, shattered, and tattered

The deepest things I do not know

And they are of no concern today

I know you loved us and I was your oldest son

I did not know why you cheated on Dad

Or drank and left us for extended periods of time

But, today I can imagine the pain and torment you experienced

Ma you did the best you could with what you knew

And you had a love for me I'll never forget

I didn't comprehend why you chose cards and drinking

Over taking us out or being with us

But, if I think about it like Jesus you were there

At my sporting events, at my rescue, in time of trouble

You could only be Ma and not Dad

Thank you, baby, thank you, Ma

I love you, Ma and I forgive you with unconditional love

Ma, I would not trade you for anything

I love you, Ma

I do not harbor any wrongs and forgive me Ma

I'm saved today and blessed and thankful

For Jesus and you

March 22, 2002

Speak Dad

Son, my eldest son

Please understand that I taught you

Only and only what I knew

My life was full of hidden trauma and drama

My dad dictated and communicated not

Your mother and I knew not love

We were bound by generational snares

Coming forth out of plantation bondage

Learning to be parents by observation only

Oh yea, son I need to admit

No, I was not with you in body

But with you in Spirit always

See I was strong outwardly

Inside I was heartbroken, hurt, weak, and lonely

My parents in my time shared feeling no

They were deeply hidden and suppressed

So oldest son, know within your heart

Love was prevalent then and now

Be taught as well as teach

Stay open-minded, in weak, in pain

Realize growth rises from them all

As you write, feel, express, talk

Know Dad also, love also, human also

March 22, 2002

About The Author

Richard H. Harris Jr. is a self-motivated baby boomer whose life in basic and fundamental education; the streets, prison, and college inspired his writing. His familial upbringing and relationships emotionally would shift along with his substance abuse issues. He subsequently entered the prison system for the first time at 43 years old battered, shattered, and tattered. After his release in 2000 he would enter college, successfully complete his 1 year parole plan, obtain an Associate in Applied Science A.A.S. degree (Human Services), be Licensed by the State of Ohio as a Ordained Minister, complete his Bachelor of Social Work B.S.W. Degree, and receive his Masters in Pastoral Counseling M.P.C. degree in late 2008.

His self-confidence and passion to help others attain their greatest God given potential is the aspiration. Accomplishing this objective through his onerous life style using Scripture, techniques, and theories created to align with ones spiritual being; there for resulting in lifelong change. Elder Harris's philosophy is "one has a choice to be better or bitter" regardless of the circumstances.

Mr. Harris is a Ordained Minister Social Worker Help Care Professional, Teacher & Motivational Speaker. Elder Harries has five sons, a daughter, 10 grandchildren and one great grandson.

Edwards Brothers Malloy
Thorofare, NJ USA
January 13, 2016